KHANIQUAHI-NIMATULLAHI (NIMATULLAHI SUFI ORDER)

306 West 11th Street
New York, New York 10014
Tel: 212-924-7739

4021 19th Avenue
San Francisco, California 94132
Tel: 415-586-1313

4931 MacArthur Blvd. NW
Washington, D.C. 20007
Tel: 202-338-4757

84 Pembroke Street
Boston, Massachusetts 02118
Tel: 617-536-0076

310 NE 57th Street
Seattle, Washington 98105
Tel: 206-527-5018

11019 Arleta Avenue
Mission Hills, Los Angeles
California 91345
Tel: 818-365-2226

4642 North Hermitage
Chicago, Illinois 60640
Tel: 312-561-1616

405 Greg Avenue
Santa Fe, New Mexico 87501
Tel: 505-983-8500

219 Chace Street
Santa Cruz, California 95060
Tel: 408-425-8454

41 Chepstow Place
London W2 4TS, England
Tel: 01-229-0769

THE GREAT SATAN 'EBLIS'

Also available by Dr. Javad Nurbakhsh:

1. In the Tavern of Ruin: Seven Essays on Sufism
2. In the Paradise of the Sufis
3. What the Sufis Say
4. Masters of the Path
5. Divani Nurbakhsh: Sufi Poetry
6. Sufism: Meaning, Knowledge and Unity
7. Sufism: Fear and Hope, Contraction and Expansion, Gathering and Dispersion, Intoxication and Sobriety, Annihilation and Subsistence
8. Traditions of the Prophet: Vol.I
9. Traditions of the Prophet: Vol.II
10. Sufi Women
11. The Truths of Love: Sufi Poetry
12. Jesus in the Eyes of the Sufis
13. Spiritual Poverty in Sufism
14. Sufism III
15. Sufi Symbolism I: The Nurbakhsh Encyclopedia of Sufi Terminology

THE GREAT SATAN 'EBLIS'

BY
DR. JAVAD NURBAKHSH

KHANIQAHI-NIMATULLAHI PUBLICATIONS
LONDON

Translated under the supervision of Dr. Javad Nurbakhsh by Terry Graham in collaboration with Neil Johnston, Sima Johnston and Barry McCutcheon. Design by Jane Lewisohn.

British Library Cataloguing in Publication Data

THE GREAT SATAN
'Eblis'
1. Persian literature — 747 1500 — Translations into English
2. English literature — Translations into Persian
3. Devil — Literary collections.
I. Nurbakhsh, Javad
II. Shatân-e Bezork "Eblis".
English
891'5508'0382 PK6449.E1
ISBN 0-933546-23-8

Published by Khaniqahi-Nimatullahi Publications
London
41 Chepstow Place
London W2 4TS
Great Britain
Tel: 01-229-0769

Printed by Morning Litho Printers in Great Britain.

CONTENTS

ABBREVIATIONS

The following system of initials indicating the titles of standard reference works on Sufism has been adopted for the sake of brevity. Where page numbers are not indicated, the reference in question is a lexical work, organised in the form of alphabetically ordered entries. The full bibliographical details of these titles may be found at the back of the book.

B	*Bustân*
EE	*Estelâḥât-e 'Erâqi*
EK(J)	*Ketâb-e ensân-e kâmel* (Jili)
EK(N)	*Ketâb-e ensân-e kâmel* (Nasafi)
EN	*Elâhi-nâma*
HA	*Haft aurang*
JA	*Rasâ'el jâme' Anṣâri*
KAM	*Kashf al-asrâr* (Maibodi)
KM	*Kashf al-maḥjub*
KST	*Kholâṣa-ye sharḥ-e ta'arrof*
MA	*Majmu'a-ye âthâr-e-fârsi-ye Aḥmad Ghazâli*
MM	*Mathnawi-ye ma'nawi*
MN	*Moṣibat-nâma*
MT	*Manṭeq-o'ṭ-ṭair*
NAQ	*Nâmahâ-ye 'Aino'l-Qoḍhât-e Hamadâni*
OK	*Osul-e kâfi*
RQ	*Resâla-ye Qoshairiya*
RSh	*Resâlahâ-ye Shâh Ne'mato'llâh Wali*
S	*Sahwâneh*
SS	*Sharḥ-e shaṭḥiyât* (Ruzbehân)
T	*Tamhidât*
TA	*Tadhkerat al-auliyâ'*
TH	*Ṭawâsin* (Ḥallâj)

INTRODUCTION

IN THE NAME OF THE TRANSCENDENT THE SACRED

The Sufis have adopted contrasting approaches to Eblis [Satan] in their works, sometimes giving him a station worthy of esteem and commendation, and at other times ostracizing him.

Among the Sufi masters, Ḥallâj, Aḥmad Ghazâli and the disciples of the latter have presented a particular view of Eblis, stressing the importance of his rank and noble-mindedness.

I have put this brief work together in the hope of providing answers which might be helpful to those who are curious to know exactly what the Sufis mean in their presentations of Eblis, with the possibility that the scope of their own ideas of Eblis may be broadened at the same time. Since Eblis is, from one point of view, 'the father of the devils', and from another, in the opinion of a number of great figures on the Path, a man of stature in the way of Divine Unity (*tauḥid)*, and the noblest of the noble, I have named him 'The Great Satan', hence the title of the book.

WHO IS EBLIS?

Eblis was one of the intimate angels of the court of God, worshipping Him for thousands of years (seven hundred thousand years by his own account)[1]. God created Eblis of fire

1. MAG 11-12

and man of earth. When God created Adam he commanded the angels to bow down before him. All prostrated themselves except for Eblis, who refused, thus disobeying God's command. God expelled him from the court of nearness to Himself, causing him to be accursed until the Final Day.

Up to the time when Eblis was expelled by God, his name was 'Azâzil and he was supreme among the angels, but, because of his disobedience, God renamed him 'Eblis'. Because Eblis saw Adam as the cause of his being cursed, he swore before God that he would work to drive Adam's children away from God, and lead them astray. Eblis is the father of the devils who exert influence over the children of Adam.

THE ORIGIN OF "EBLIS"

Primitive man believed in a multitude of deities of virtues and vices, ascribing a god to each good or evil manifestation of nature. The religion of Zoroaster [the ancient prophet of the Persians] taught that the essence of power and knowledge and the fountainhead of goodness, veracity, holiness and piety was called Ahurâ Mazdâ, while the source of evil, vileness, abomination, darkness, ignorance and cruelty was called 'Ahriman'.

In the Semitic religions (Judaism, Christianity and Islam) the power of Ahriman as a being independent of God was reduced, such that he was considered to be a creation of the Unique Godhead, albeit a disobedient and rebellious creation which did possess a certain amount of power. God called him 'Eblis'.

Sufis found this representation of Eblis to be inconsistent with the school of Divine Unity and the creed of the unity of being (*waḥdat-e wojud*). In rejecting the Semitic representation they appeared opposed to religion, and so created problems for themselves.

In order to prove their adherence to Divine Unity, they had to address themselves to the problem of Eblis. Their consequent approach was, on the one hand, to repudiate the concept of absolute evil, positing that evil is relative, and on the other, to assert that the Unique Godhead possesses both wrath and grace, as well as beauty and majesty, and that Eblis is one of the manifestations of God's majesty.

O you who have heard that there is no evil from him,
the truth is that there is no such thing as a malicious being.
If the mirror of your heart is tarnished, an ugly
person will appear as beautiful as an angel.

Sabzawâri

Both those Sufi masters who sympathised with Eblis, considering him a true lover, and those who opposed him, regarding him as an impure traveller on the path, presented him as impotent and powerless. This caused them to lose interest in Eblis, and considering him to be utterly insignificant, they were free to devote themselves exclusively to the Unique Godhead, peerless and omnipotent.

SEIZING THE 'PEN' FROM THE ENEMY'S HAND

Sa'di in his Bustân relates the following story, in verse, about Eblis.

I do not know in which book I read
That someone saw Eblis in a dream.

He appeared angelic, like a stately pine;
A light, like the sun, was radiating from his face.

The dreamer went to meet him and exclaimed,
"Amazing! Is that you? No angel has such fairness!

With a face like this, beauteous as the moon,
Why are you known in the world as being ugly?

Why did the artist in the palace of the king
Draw a visage so gloomy, grotesque and ravaged?"

When that benighted devil heard these words,
He wailed and shrieked,

Crying, "O fortunate one! This isn't my real form!
Why is it that the pen is in the hand of my enemy!"

BI

In this book we have given the pen to the great Sufi gnostics so that they may tell the story of Eblis for you in their own words.

THE GREAT SATAN 'EBLIS'

THE REFUSAL TO PROSTRATE WAS ACCORDING TO GOD'S DECREE AND WILL

Certain of the Sufi masters believe that Eblis' refusal to bow down before Adam was predisposed by the pre-eternal decree and will of God. Eblis did not prostrate because God did not want it. These masters consider the cause of Eblis' disobedience to have been God's will, not his own desire. To illustrate this, let us cite some examples of their writings on this subject.

* * *

According to Aḥmad Ghazâli, "the pre-existing favour is the seed of post-eternal bliss, while the lack of effort on our part is the seed of post-eternal damnation. This rule applies to all. Before Adam was created and was disobedient, the designation of the 'Eternal' prepared the 'arc of choice' for him, so that he would find post-eternal salvaton; so, his Lord chose him and established repentance for him, providing guidance for him.

This benighted one [Eblis] was amongst the misguided before the creation.

What are the relative positions of these two? Both were presented to Destiny's banker. He declared that their coin be submitted to the touchstone of sin and devotion. The wretched

Eblis turned out to be counterfeit and was consigned to the foundry, while Adam, being genuine, was turned over to the treasury of the king.

MAG 41

God commanded Eblis, "Prostrate before Adam!", while desiring that he should not do so. Hence, he did not.

KM 324

O God, if Eblis misguided Adam, who then provided him with wheat for his daily bread?

JA 30

Let me speak plainly and not be afraid. Is the duck afraid of the water in a deluge? And what difference does it make to a swimmer if the ship sinks or not? Joseph secretly told Benjamin one thing, while publicly accusing him of theft, and exposing him to degradation before both worlds; and Benjamin was content throughout. Take note! Take note! "Verily in Joseph and his brethren are signs [of God's sovereignty] for the enquiring." (Koran XII:7) Now having heard a fiction in this context, pay heed to what lies behind the apparent censure of Benjamin so that you may understand what God told Eblis inwardly, and why, when Eblis was content, God consequently shamed him outwardly. "And indeed, My curse is upon you..." (Koran XXXVIII:78). And Eblis said:

> I have a soul which bears the burden of your love;
>   as long as I have this soul,
> I shall not cease to sacrifice myself in your service.

For him there is no thought of anyone but God.

NAQ 189

What choice has a piece of iron which is subjected to magnetic attraction but to be drawn to the surface thereof? What choice has the moth which has become enamoured of the fire but to hurl itself upon the fire? God told Adam and Eve, "... And do not approach this tree..." (II:35), and He ordered the tree to stay close to Adam so that he would not be forgetful of it for a single moment, "... And God is the best of schemers." (III:54, VIII:30) God told Eblis inwardly whatever He told him; what do you suppose that was? There is no one in heaven or earth who can follow up this matter unless God wills it. Then He told him outwardly, "Prostrate!" The poor fellow was forced, according to what was commanded of him inwardly to say, "Shall I fall prostrate before that which you have created of clay?" (XVII:61). To which God said, "And indeed my curse is upon you..." (XXXVIII:78) Eblis could only say, "The robe of honour is conferred by you, whether it attracts your curse or your mercy." Eblis saw all mankind, from first to last, as merely children on the path to God.

How eloquently Ḥosain Manṣur Ḥallâj puts it in his *Tawâsin!* "The quality of chivalry can be ascribed only to Eblis and Aḥmad [Moḥammad]. O Lord, I do not worship you for the sake of mercy; I maintain no condition for my devotion. I am content with whatever you will and whatever you do; while others seek to avoid your curse, I make it the crown on my head and the blazon on my sleeve."

What committed aspiration (*hemmat*)! He said, "I am ready for the post-eternal pain; may You be endlessly merciless for my sake."

Adam's people have heard the name of Eblis, but I know that for him there is no thought of any individual, for he is subjected to post-eternal pain. His sustenance is the curse that affects him continuously, and he drinks it just as God's friends do His mercy. In fact, he despises mercy more than the friends despise that curse. What do the people of the world know of this?

NAQ 186-8

If you do not know what the 'My' of "And, indeed, My curse is upon you," (XXXVIII:78) means, I am not surprised. By that majesty and grandeur of God who subsists in Himself, there is not one moment which passes where the 'My' of 'My curse' withholds sustenance from Eblis. O dear friends, as long as Eblis exists, everything he does is by the decree of the 'My' of 'My curse'. He does nothing which is not commanded directly by God. God told him, in a way that reached the ears of Gabriel and Michael, "... Fall ye prostrate before Adam..." (VII:11), whereas in the sanctum of the sanctum, He told him, "Do not prostrate to what is other than me."

You've tied me to a board and thrown me into the sea;
Yet you tell me, "Be careful! Don't get wet!"

Moreover, he threw the Friend's curse over his shoulder like a black mantle, as a keepsake, and departed from 'you-ness', to enter that which is 'I-ness'.

NAQ 411

God created Eblis, 'the outcast', from fire, giving him a place by the 'farthest lote-tree' (LIII:14). He sent his intimates to study with him, and kept him in the station of service for a hundred thousand years until he bound the cincture of the curse around his waist. He shaped earthy Adam out of dark clay and, without subjecting him to service, placed the crown of esteem and preference upon his head. They asked, "Why this esteem and pre-eminence for Adam, and that humiliation and hopelessness for Eblis?" God replied, "We have apportioned..." (XLIII:31); concerning Our apportionment there is no why or wherefore.

KAM IX 76

Externally Adam committed an error and Eblis a sin. God said to Adam, "Do not eat the grain of wheat," and he ate it. He said to Eblis, "Prostrate!" and he did not do so. However their acceptance or rejection was not based upon their actions, but on that which flows from the 'Pen'[1], and the decrees of the Eternal. The 'Pen', as a consequence of the will of the Eternal Being inscribed fortune in Adam's case; and within his nature a greater steadfastness was created and the order of forgiveness was issued for his sin saying, "(We made a covenant with Adam in ancient times) but he forgot and we found no constancy in him." (XX:115) As for Eblis, the 'Pen' had inscribed expulsion and failure through the Eternal Being. God set an ambush within his nature and apportioned sin for him saying, "...he refused and was proud and became one of the unbelievers." (II:34) Because of the decree of pre-eternal rejection, God fashioned a collar from His curse, and placed it around the neck of Eblis' destiny. Every substance which emerged from the crucible of his actions became dross in the hands of the assayer of 'Knowledge', that is to say, impure. His devotion became the cause of his accursedness, his worship the reason for his expulsion. The reality of his action indicates that the divine decree is not to be questioned, the pre-eternal is not to be contested.

KAM VIII 373

Emâm Ja'far Ṣâdeq said, "Sometimes God makes a command that he does not wish to be obeyed, and sometimes he wants that which he has forbidden. He ordered Eblis to prostrate himself before Adam, while desiring him not to do so, for if he had so desired, Eblis would have done so. He forbade Adam to eat of the tree, while desiring him to do so, whereas if he had not desired, Adam would not have eaten thereof.

OK I 276

1. Koran LXVIII:1, XCVI:4. Ḥallâj equates the 'Pen' with the 'total reality' and al-Fârâbi equates it with 'the Spirit', 'the Intellect'. L. Massignon, *The Passion of Ḥallâj: Mystic and Martyr of Islam*. Translated from French by H. Mason (Princeton University Press, 1982), Vol. 1, p. 381, Vol. 2, p. 122.

When God breathed that pure soul into Adam's frame of water and earth,

He did not want any of the angels to be aware that Adam had that soul.

"Spiritual ones of heaven," he commanded, "prostrate yourselves forthwith in front of Adam."

They all bowed down their heads upon the earth; none was aware of that pure secret.

Eblis' turn came, "No one will see my prostration at this moment," he said.

"Even if they tear my head from my body, I'll have no regret, for I'll still have my neck.[1]

I know that Adam is not clay; I am not afraid of losing my head to see the secret."

Since Eblis lay in ambush, head unbowed, he saw the secret.

The Exalted One spoke, "O you spy of the Way, you have secretly seen this station of Adam.

Since you have seen the treasure that I have hidden I must kill you, so you can't reveal it to the world.

For no matter where the king conceals the treasure, it is never hidden from his guard.

For the one before whose eyes it is placed, life's line is drawn, and without doubt, he will die.

O man who has chosen to see a treasure, you must be ready to lose your head.

If I do not cut your head from your body now, you'll reveal the secret to the world."

Eblis replied, "O Lord, spare this slave! Have pity on this wretch you have driven out!"

Almighty God declared, "I'll grant you respite, I've placed the collar of my curse around your neck.

I shall write your name as the 'Great Liar', and you will stand accused until the Resurrection."

Thereupon Eblis said, "Why should I fear that curse, since that pure treasure has been revealed to me?

1. The neck that has not bowed down to anyone but God.

That curse is yours, that mercy is yours; the slave is yours, and his portion is yours.

If it is my portion to be cursed, I am not afraid, for poison must exist as well as the antidote.

When I see the world seeking your curse, I withhold it, for I am impudent.

If you wish to be a seeker, you must seek like this, otherwise you are not seeking; you are grasping.

If you fail to find him, seeking day and night, it is not that he is lost, it is your deficient seeking.

'Aṭṭâr MT 181

Then it became certain; He who exalts whom he wills, commanded a thing of clay to spread forth its wings.

He commanded a thing of fire, "Go, become Eblis; go down with your deceit beneath the earth's seventh layer.

Earthy Adam, rise up to the heavens; Eblis of fire, plunge down to the earth.

There is no reason for my action; it is direct; I ordain; there is no reason, O infirm one.

I reverse my practise at the appointed time; I cause the dust that I stirred up, to settle down.

I bid the sea, 'Be full of fire!' and tell the fire, 'Become a garden!' "

Rumi MM II 1622-7

If your slate is so clean, why did you create Satan?

You say that one should not pay attention to Satan's wicked words;

Yet you've given him refuge in my skin and veins, so he can wink and encourage me to do bad deeds.

You order us to do our devotions and Satan to run wild in our body and soul.

You create a commotion, so the deer may flee; then spur on the hound to pursue the chase!

I have much to say, but I do not dare; I am so frightened, I cannot even breathe.

Nâser Khosrau

EBLIS' OWN ACCOUNT OF THE REASON FOR HIS DISOBEDIENCE

Various Sufi masters, seeing Eblis with either the inner or outer eye, have asked him why he disobeyed, and have reported his reply in his own words.

God wanted to make of me a symbol of cursedness;
He did what he wanted and used Adam merely as an
excuse.

Sanâ'i

According to Ḥallâj, Moses met Eblis on the slopes of Sinai and asked him, "What stopped you from prostrating?" Eblis explained, "My claim is that I was worshipping 'the Unique Object'. If I had prostrated before Adam, I would have been like you. When God told you once to look at the mountain, you did so, but when God told me a thousand times to prostrate before Adam, I refused. That claim was my spiritual reality." "You disregarded the command," Moses said. "That was a test," replied Eblis, "not a command." "But your form changed," Moses countered. "O Moses," said Eblis, "that was a deception; here is the real Eblis. A state is not to be relied upon, because it changes, whereas gnosis is correct, remaining as it is, even if the individual changes." "Do you remember Him now?" Moses asked. "O Moses," said Eblis, "one does not remember remembrance;"[1] I am remembered as He is remembered.

1. He is so present that there is no question of 'remembering Him'.

Remembrance of Him is remembrance of me, his
remembrance is mine;
How can two remember one another unless they are
one?

"Now, my service is purer, my time is sweeter, and my remembrance more sublime, for I served him for my own pleasure in pre-eternity, and now I serve him for his. I have done away with craving, prohibition and repulsion, harm and benefit, all have disappeared. He made me alone, driving me until I forsook the company of others. I was kept from others because of my partiality, changed because of my consternation, confounded through my banishment, estranged from God through my service, an outlaw because of my words, deprecated because of my eulogising, distanced from God through my separation, separated from God through my contemplative vision, exposed through my union, drawn to him because of my severance, and cut off from him to negate my egoism. In being true to him I have not erred in what he ordained; I have not denied his ordainment. I have not been concerned by the change of form. If he consigns me to torment in the fire for an eternity of eternities, I will not prostrate before other than him, nor abase myself before anyone. I shall not know other than him. My claim is that of the sincere; I am one of the sincere ones amongst the lovers.

TH 45-49

Encountering Eblis on the slopes of Sinai, Moses hailed him and asked, "O Eblis, why did you not prostrate before Adam?" Eblis replied, "Heaven forbid that anyone worship anything but the One. For seven hundred thousand years I have been saying, 'Praise be the All Holy.' Do you expect me to spoil my devotion with dualism?" "Then why did you not obey God's command?" Moses asked. "This command was a test," replied Eblis, "if he had really intended to give me a command, I would have said that I am an adherent of Divine Unity."

Even if I were cut to pieces
I would not attach my heart to another.[1]

"You wanted to look at God. He said, 'Look at me' and you looked at the mountain. As God is my judge, if you had not looked at the mountain, you would have seen him. In unity I am more truthful than you." "Without a doubt," said Moses, "you have lost your senses!" "Ah, Moses," Eblis answered, "this depends on the Judge and his inclination. The fact is my unity is beyond question." "But your form was transmuted from that of an angel to that of the devil," said Moses. "This is a state," replied Eblis, "which changes." "O Eblis," said Moses, "do you love God?" He replied, "Every time his love increases towards someone else, my love and devotion increases towards him." "O Eblis," said Moses, "do you remember him?" He answered, "I am the one remembered by him, to whom he said, 'My curse be upon you!' Do not the 'you' and the 'I' coexist in that curse? I am pledged to loving and yearning. I am in heaven and hell." "O Eblis," said Moses, "how is it that despite your cursed existence, your words are sweet? Speak." "My experiences," replied Eblis, "are those of one who has been tested, Moses. I worshipped God for seven hundred thousand years, craving a better position with him, and this craving in devotion brings about destruction. I stopped craving, and now my remembrance is keener, my devotion sweeter. O Moses, do you know why God has caused me to be separated? So that I would not mix with the sincere ones, and worship him out of passion or fear or hope or craving [in order that Eblis would not compete with others in his worship].

MAG 11-12

Bâyazid Basṭâmi said, "I asked God if he would present Eblis to me. I found him in the sacred enclosure [at Mecca]. I engaged him in conversation.

'O wretch,' I said, 'being so cunning, why did you ignore the command of God?' 'Ah, Bâyazid,' he replied, 'that command was a test, not a command to be obeyed. If it had

1. Verse ascribed to Ebrâhim Adham.

been, I would never have ignored it.' 'O wretch,' I said, 'it was your opposition to God which brought you to this condition.' 'Not at all, O Bâyazid,' he answered, 'opposition arises from the conflict of opposites, and God has no opposite. Agreement, on the other hand, arises from the relation of like with like, and God has no like. It may seem that agreement came from me when I was in agreement, and that opposition came from me when I was in opposition, but both come from God, because no one has power before Him. Despite all that has passed, I still have hope in the mercy of Him who said, "And my mercy embraces all things" (VII:156), for I am a thing.' I said, 'This is based on the condition of one's piety.' 'No,' he said, 'the condition is advocated by one who is ignorant of the outcome of things, but He is the Lord, from whom nothing is hidden.' At that Eblis disappeared from sight."

KAM I 161

Sahl 'Abdo'llâh Tostari related, "One day I came upon Eblis, and said, 'I seek refuge in God from you.' 'O Sahl,' he replied, 'while you have sought refuge in God from me, I have sought refuge from God in God. O Sahl, if you say, 'God protect me from the hand of Satan'. I say, 'God protect me from the hand of the merciful.' 'O Eblis,' I asked, 'Why did you not prostrate before Adam?' 'O Sahl,' he answered, 'spare me such futile questions. If you have access to the Divine Presence, ask, 'If you do not want this wretch, why do you keep making excuses for him?' O Sahl, just now I was standing on Adam's grave. A thousand times I prostrated upon it, pressing the earth upon my eyes. Finally, I heard a voice crying, 'Do not trouble yourself, for We do not want you.' "

KAM I 160

Jonaid is reported to have said he wanted to see Eblis. "I was standing in the mosque, when I saw an old man who approached me from afar. I grew frightened at the sight of him and asked who he was. 'You asked to see me,' he replied. 'O cursed one,' I said, 'what kept you from prostrating before Adam?' 'O Jonaid,' he answered, 'how could you imagine that I would prostrate before what is other than God?' I was confounded by what he said. A voice came to my inner consciousness, counselling, 'Say: you are lying, if you were a devotee, you would have obeyed God's command, you would not have rebelled against it and incurred His prohibition." On hearing these words repeated by Jonaid, Eblis howled, and cried, "By God, you have burned me!" Whereupon he disappeared.

TA 426

It has been recounted that when he came to Adam, Eblis said, "Know that you have been given a clean slate and I a dirty one, but don't be so sure of yourself, for our situation is like that of the husbandman who tends the almond tree in the orchard till it bears fruit, when he takes the almonds to the market and sells them. One customer is happy and another mournful. The mournful one blackens the almonds and strews them over a coffin in his dead, while the happy one coats them with sugar and scatters them as sweets at his festivities. O Adam, I am that blackened almond that is strewn over coffins and you are the one which is scattered on joyful occasions. However, you must know that the husbandman of both is the same, and that we have both drunk from the same stream. If one is in contact with flowers, he is steeped in their aroma, and if one is in contact with thorns, the eyes are scratched by them."

KAM I 160

Ebrâhim Khawâṣṣ related, "Being in complete solitude (*tajrid*) in the desert, I encountered an old man wearing a hat, sitting in an isolated spot, and crying his eyes out. I asked, 'You there, who are you?' 'I am the Devil,' he replied. 'Why are you crying,' I asked. 'Who deserves to cry more than I? I served that court for forty thousand years and there was no one higher than me in the empyrean realms. Now, look at what the divine command and decree of the Unseen have wreaked upon me!'

Then he said, 'O Khawâṣṣ, look well, so that you may not be deceived into such effort and devotion as mine, for everything depends upon God's favour and discretion, not on the effort and devotion of the devotee. I was commanded to prostrate before Adam and I did not do so; Adam was ordered not to eat from that tree yet he did so. Favour was at work in Adam's case; God forgave him, saying, "(We made a covenant with Adam in ancient times) but he forgot and we found no constancy in him," (XX:115). Whereas in my case, favour was withheld, and God said, "He refused and was proud..." (II:34). Adam's error was not counted, while my sustained devotion went for nought.' "

KAM X 134

Shebli related that Eblis came to him and said, "Beware lest the exhilaration of the moment blind you to the afflictions of the plague which lurks behind them."

TA 622

Sahl ebn 'Abdo'llâh related, "I encountered Eblis and I recognised him. He knew that I recognised him. A conversation ensued. I had my say, and he had his. The talk grew heated, leading to a dispute which went on and on, until we both stopped. I was at a loss and so was he. One of the last things he said to me was, 'O Sahl, God said, "... And my Mercy embraces all things..." (VII:156) This is the general case. I am sure you are aware that I am a 'thing', and God's statement presupposes that everything is embraced, even the most hideous of things. Therefore his mercy extends to me as well.' "

Sahl continued, "I swear by God, that the grace and power of expression that Eblis displayed in interpreting this verse dumbfounded me! He understood something in it that had evaded my understanding, he knew something about the guidance provided by the verse that I had failed to perceive. I was left stunned and pensive. I began to study that verse in my heart until I reached the words, '... therefore I shall ordain it (mercy) for those who ward off evil...' (VII:156). I was delighted! I imagined I had found victory in the argument, and that I could break Eblis' back with this revelation. I said to him,

'O cursed one, God has limited the general statement by declaring, "...I shall ordain it for those who ward off evil...".

Eblis smiled and said, 'O Sahl, I do not think you so ignorant, nor do I believe you are serious in this. Did it never occur to you, O Sahl, that the limitation is yours, not God's?[1]

I understood; I was confounded; saliva stuck in my throat. I swear by God I could find no answer nor could I close the door upon him. I knew that he craved something, namely, mercy.

He went his way and I went mine. I swear by God, I have no idea what will happen in the future for God has given no indication of the resolution of this ambiguity. I was left without any understanding as to what God's will was in creating Satan. I cannot give an opinion as to whether God's decree concerning him has terminated or not, for when God broadens his decree he does not narrow it again; however, he has apportioned different ways for his devotees to follow. He bestows grace upon one group in one way and upon another in another. One cannot circumscribe God's intention with respect to anything, for he transcends any such attempt; God's mercy towards the devout is a necessary part of his divinity, that which he has made requisite upon himself, while his mercy towards the non-devout is a part of his benevolence and grace, just as piety of the devout is a part of benevolence and grace. Thus, the court of God's mercy embraces everything.

Sharḥ-e kalamât-e ṣufiya 204

The following verses depict Eblis' own description of his downfall:

My heart was one with him in love and sympathy; my heart was the nest for the Simorgh of love.

The host of angels was the army of my court; the Mighty Throne was my threshold.

God hid his snare of deceit in my path; Adam was the bait in that snare.

God wanted to make me a symbol of cursedness; he did as he willed and used Adam as the excuse.

1. God's mercy is not limited to the pious alone.

I was the teacher of the angels in the heavenly realm; my hope, to remain forever in sublime eternity.

I spent seven hundred thousand years in devotion; my devotion filled a thousand thousand treasuries.

On the Guarded Tablet I read that there would be one accursed; I suspected everyone else, but not myself.

Adam was of clay; I was of the purest light; I said I was unique but it was he who was unique.

The angels said, 'You didn't prostrate!' How could I have done so when I did what he had ordained for me?

O soul, come, do not depend upon your devotions; this verse is for the insight of the people of the world.

Finally I knew what destiny brought me; a hundred springs flowed from these two eyes.

O rationalists of love, I, too have no sin; one cannot find the path to God without his satisfaction.

Sanâ'i

One evening Moses went to Sinai; Eblis came to him from afar.

Thus he asked that cursed one, "O you who are so boastful, why did you not prostrate before Adam?"

The cursed one said, "O you accepted by God, I found myself rejected without reason before his power.

If there had been a way for me to prostrate, I would have been 'God's conversant'[1], like you.

But since God wished me to speak awry, thus it came to be."

Moses said, "O you, trapped in yourself, did you never remember God?"

Eblis replied, "Since I am a lover, I could never forget him, even for a moment.

As much as his wrath increases towards me, my love increases towards him."

1. A reference to Moses' epithet, derived from the Koran, *Kalimo'llâh*.

Although the cursed one is far from God's precincts, he is, in Moses' words, in the presence of God.

Although the curse burned his heart, that curse itself, increased his yearning.

Since Satan is so fervent on the path, how, then, are you in your love of the Beloved?

'Aṭṭâr

An incomparable one said, "Travelling in the desert, I saw two black streams flowing.

I followed them in order to discover their source, noting the while how rapid was their flow.

Finally, when I came to a rock, I saw Eblis lying on the ground.

His eyes like two clouds, were pouring forth blood; from each of his eyes a bloody stream flowed.

His tears fell like the rain; he wailed, repeating this refrain,

'My story has nothing to do with God, but the colour of my destiny is black.

Since no one wants my obedience they place the burden of sin on my back.

To whom else has such a thing ever happened? No one has ever had a story like mine!' "

'Aṭṭâr EN 104

Now Shebli, that Imam, igniter of the world, was walking on 'Arafât[1] one day.

Suddenly his eye fell on Eblis. He called out, "O cursed one of God's court!

Since you have no Islam and possess no devotion, why are you wandering around amongst the pilgrims.

Burning with regret over your blackened fortune? Do you still hope for divine reprieve?"

1. Ritual stopping place for the pilgrims at Mecca.

When Eblis, full of grief, had heard these words he cried, "O Shaikh of the world!

For hundreds of thousands of years I worshipped God, between fear and hope.

I showed the angels the way to the divine presence, I guided every wanderer to the divine precincts.

My heart swelled with God's grandeur; I testified to his uniqueness.

Given all of this, I was suddenly, and without cause, driven from his court.

None dared to question as to why such a courtier was expelled so precipitously.

If God accepts me, again without cause, it will be no surprise; it would be a secret I could not reveal.

Since my expulsion had no cause his summons will also be without cause.

Since there is no how or why in God's work, it is unworthy to lose hope in him.

Since his wrath commanded me to go, it would be no wonder if his grace called me back."

'Aṭṭâr EN 294-5

Someone asked Eblis, "O wretched one, when it became apparent that you had been cursed,

Why did you accept it so wholeheartedly, hiding it in your heart like a treasure?"

Eblis replied, "A curse is the King's arrow, before he fires it he looks to the target;

If you have eyes, look at the archers attention to the target, not at his arrow."[1]

'Aṭṭâr EN 109

1. Eblis' only concern was God's attention to himself.

The son of 'Emrân[1] with a heart drowned in light set out for Mount Sinai for communion with God.

On the way he encountered the chief of the age, the commander of the army of the separated.[2]

Moses said, "Why were you not content to prostrate before Adam. Tell the truth!"

Eblis said, "The lover who has completed the path does not prostrate to other than God."

Moses said, "Whoever is devoted to the Friend obeys his commands wholeheartedly."

Eblis said, "The object of that exchange was to test the lover and did not call for prostration."

Moses said, "If that's the case, why is it the custom to curse and blame you?

After all, because of the King's wrath, your angelic garments became those of a devil."

Eblis said, "Both of these qualities are borrowed and are separate from the angelic essence.

A hundred qualities may come and go but my essence will not change.

My essence remains as it has always been; my essence is inseparable from my love of God.

Up to this time my love had been alloyed, dependent upon my own inclinations.

It was subject to the vicissitudes of fortune, my every moment was affected by fear and hope.

Now I have been freed from his fluctuation for I have settled down in faith.

Grace and wrath have become the same to me; mountain and molehill weigh the same to me.

Love has washed my heart clean of passion; I am only concerned with love for love."

Jâmi HA 480

1. Moses.
2. Eblis.

In the light of the foregoing selections, indicating that the cause of Eblis' disobedience was the pre-eternal will of God, the question arises as to whether human error is due to God's pre-eternal will, and if this were so, can there be any punishment in the hereafter. Similarly, if God's guidance relates to pre-eternal favour, where then is the need for human striving and effort. We do not accept such reasoning, to do so we would have to reject the very basis of religion. We maintain that such arguments are in themselves satanic. How can one agree that God's will leads one astray and then subjects one to eternal damnation on that account? Is not such action far removed from divine justice?

THE POWER OF GOD AND THAT OF EBLIS

Sufis have made various comparisons between Eblis' power and God's.

What do you say concerning his refusal to prostrate?
Was it predestined or was it a matter of choice?
If it was in his hands, then God is deficient;
And if his hands were tied, then God must be cruel!

Sanâ'i

It is related that a determinist told a Zoroastrian that he should become a Moslem. The latter replied, "If God wants that." The determinist said, "God wants that, but Satan will not let you, for he does not want it." "That's an amazing situation," said the Zoroastrian, "both God and Satan have will, but Satan's prevails over God's." ... the Zoroastrian said, "Then I shall follow the stronger protagonist, for what would I do with the weak one?"

KAM VI 234, 681

EBLIS' LACK OF INFLUENCE ON THE MASTERS OF THE PATH AND MEN OF GOD

Through a wealth of stories, Sufis have implied that the problem of Satan exists only for the ordinary people. They have indicated that Satan has no place in the affairs of the men of God; indeed they have even suggested that he may not exist at all. We present below several illustrations of this position.

When Bâyazid Basṭâmi was asked about his relationship with Eblis, he said, "Our neighbours are relieved of his temptations due to our aura; for thirty years Eblis has not had the power to set foot in our confines. 'As for My bondsmen, you have no power over them...' (XV:42)"

KAM III 55

Ebrâhim Khawâṣṣ related, "Once, when I was lost in the desert, I encountered a fellow who put me back on the right path. When I asked who he was, he replied, 'Don't you know me? I'm that chief of the unfortunates they call "Eblis".' 'But your job is to lead people astray,' I said, 'not to set them back on the right path.' 'I lead astray those who are lost,' he said, 'but I stay close to those who are on God's path and consider the dust of their feet to be a blessing.' "

KAM VIII 56

It is related that Shebli said, "One day my foot crashed through the planks of a rickety bridge and I fell into the water below, which was very deep. A strange hand seized me and pulled me to safety. Looking at the one who had saved me I recognised that outcast from God's presence. 'O accursed of the path,' I said 'your hand is for striking, not for helping. How did this occur?' 'I strike those who deserve to be struck,' he replied, 'I suffered with Adam; I don't want to go through that again with another.' "

TA 626

One of the great gnostics, passing by the door of someone's house, saw Eblis peering in and shifting his stare from one point to another. "O accursed one, what are you doing here?" he asked. Eblis replied , "In this room there is a man of God sleeping and an ignoble man saying his prayers. I want to go in and tempt the latter, but the warning in the eye of the sleeping man prevents me."

KAM 262

'Aṭṭâr demonstrates Eblis' lack of influence over the men of God in the following passage:

> A worldly man visited a master in retreat, and complained bitterly about Eblis.
>
> "Eblis has waylaid me," he moaned, "destroying my religion with his tricks."
>
> "My dear friend," replied the gnostic, "Eblis has already been to see me.
>
> He complained of you, of suffering at your hand; he was exasperated with your oppressive ways.
>
> Eblis said, 'The world is my territory; I have nothing to do with one who is detached from the world.
>
> Tell him to set out on the Path, and relinquish this world of mine.
>
> I had firm intentions upon his religion, because he had a firm grip on my world.
>
> Whoever leaves my territory completely, I have nothing more to do with him."

MT 113

It is related that Ebrâhim Adham said, "Once I was crossing the desert [on the way to Mecca], in full trust in God. For three days I found nothing to eat or drink. Then Eblis came to me and said, 'You have given up your kingdom and all your wealth in order to go hungry on the pilgrimage? You could have travelled as easily with both.' I said, 'O God, do you assign the enemy to the friend in order to burn him? I cannot leave this desert without your help.' A voice came to me, saying, 'O Ebrâhim, whatever you have in your pocket, cast it out so that We may draw forth that which lies in the unseen.' I put my hand in my pocket and found four silver coins which I had forgotten. As soon as I had thrown them away. Eblis bolted from me and sustenance came to me from the unseen. It became clear that Eblis stays close to those who possess things of the world."

TA 122

Aḥmad ebn Khaḍhruya said to Bâyazid, "O Shaikh, I saw Eblis brought to the gallows at the entrance of your road." "Yes," replied Bâyazid, "he promised that he would never come to Basṭâm.[1] Recently he came and tempted someone who subsequently became involved in a murder. The law is that an offender is hung by the gate of the King."

TA 175

It is recounted that a gnostic, going to visit Jonaid, spied Eblis fleeing from his presence. When he was received by Jonaid, he noticed that his host was agitated, displaying anger and irritating someone. He said, "O Shaikh, I have heard that Eblis' hold on Adam's children is greater when they are in a state of anger. You are angry at this moment and yet I saw Eblis running away from you." "Have you not heard?" replied Jonaid, "Do you not know that my anger is not from myself, but comes from God? As a result Eblis never takes flight with more alacrity than when I am angry."

TA 426

1. Bâyazid's home town.

IN PRAISE OF EBLIS

HIS ADHERENCE TO DIVINE UNITY

Certain Sufis believe that Eblis did not prostrate before Adam because of his adherence to Divine Unity. He saw, recognised and desired no one but God, recognising only him and bowing before him alone.

Ebn Jauzi writes that Aḥmad Ghazâli maintained that whoever does not learn adherence to Divine Unity from Eblis, is an unbeliever.

MAG 261

Ḥallâj said, "Amongst the people of the spirit, there is no adherent to Divine Unity like Eblis."

TH 42

Sahl ebn 'Abdol'llâh Tostari said, "Seeing Eblis with a group of people and being aware of the commitment involved on his part in refusing to prostrate before Adam, I was attracted to him. When the others had departed, I told him that I would not leave him until he spoke of Divine Unity. He began and his discourse was such that if the gnostics of the age had been present, they would have all been dumbfounded."

TA 331

Although I have been driven from his court, I will never be disobedient on his path.

Since I set foot in the Beloved's way, I haven't looked anywhere except towards the Beloved.

Since I became intimate with spiritual mystery, I have not even glanced at anyone.

'Aṭṭâr MN 242

However much I'm cursed by him, I'll not submit to other than him.

If I were to look upon anything else, I would not have such power over everything in the world.

'Aṭṭâr EN 107

At the very moment when Eblis was cursed he began to pray and praise. He cried,

"A curse from you is a hundred times finer than turning from you towards anything else."

'Aṭṭâr EN 108

Ḥallâj said, "Eblis, at a time when he was not aware of anything other than himself, said, 'I am better [than Adam]'.[1] Pharaoh said to his people, 'Aside from myself, I do not know of any other God for you,' because he did not recognise that his own people could distinguish between reality and unreality. I said, 'If you do not know Him then recognise His sign. I am that sign. I am the True Reality *(ana'l-ḥaqq),* which indicates my continuous realisation of the Reality.' "

TH 50

Ḥallâj said, "God said to Eblis, 'Free will is mine, not yours.' Eblis said, 'All free will, including mine, is yours. I chose you over myself, O Creator, and when you prevented me from prostrating, you were "the Preventer". If I have erred in what I have said, do not reject me, for you are "the Hearer" (you hear what is in my heart), and if you had wanted me to prostrate before him [Adam], I would have obeyed. Amongst the gnostics, there is not one who knows you better than I."

TH 53

Ḥallâj said, "The claim of divine knowledge became indisputable only for Moḥammad and Eblis; Eblis approached the Essence but fell, while Moḥammad approached and it was revealed.

God said to Moḥammad, 'Look!' and he did not look, he turned neither right nor left. 'The eye turned not aside nor yet was overbold' (LIII:17) God said to Eblis, 'Prostrate yourself!' and he did not. Eblis claimed divine knowledge but continued acting under his own will and power.

Moḥammad said, 'It is through you that I gain strength, and through you that I attack. O Turner of Hearts! I cannot count the praises of you, only you are worthy of praising yourself.'[1]

In heaven there was no worshipper or adherent to Divine Unity like Eblis. He was confounded by the Essence, but never once did he waiver in attention to God on his spiritual journey, adoring the Beloved in his absolute aloneness (*tajrid*). He was cursed when he reached the point of isolation from himself and was driven from the door because he sought solitariness (*fardâniyat*).

When he was commanded, 'Prostrate yourself!' he said, 'Not to other [than you]'. God then said, 'My curse be upon you to the Day of Judgement;' (XXXVIII:78) and still Eblis said, 'Not to other [than you]'.

My denial is sanctification of you,
My craziness in you is my comprehension.

There is no Adam but for you,
And who is Eblis to make the distinction?

1. This statement is derived from a prophetic tradition *(ḥadith)* which is cited by Forozânfar in his *Aḥadith-e mathnawi* (Tehran 1955) No.3.

He plunged into the Sea of Divine Splendour, became blinded, and said, 'There is no way for me but you, for I am a humble lover.' God said to him 'You have become proud.' He replied, 'If I had been with you but a moment my pride would have been justified; I have been with you for centuries.' "

TH 41-2

HIS LOVE OF GOD'S WRATH

The Sufis maintain that God possesses both beauty and majesty, or, expressed differently, grace and wrath. The Sufi is one who loves both grace and wrath, not one who is gladdened by the grace and depressed by the wrath.

Eblis loved God's wrath, because, when God cursed him, he was not distraught; in fact he was gladdened by the 'My' which prefaced the curse, because it meant that the curse came from God, and whatever comes from him is welcome, as the following verses illustrate:

And that burned one, whose brilliant face
gave fieriness to fire,
Made the claim of welcoming fire shamelessly.

'Erâqi

How strange! I am in love with his grace and his
wrath,
I love these opposites to the fullest extent.

Rumi MM I 1570

Even if both worlds were to curse me
The love in my soul would remain unchanged.

'Aṭṭâr EN 105

Dho'n-Nun said, "I saw Eblis spend forty days in prostration without raising his head. I said to him, 'O wretch, since God drove you away and cursed you, what is all this devotion? He replied, 'O Dho'n-Nun, I may have been dismissed from devotion, but he has not been dismissed from Lordship.' "

KAM I 160

Just as Moḥammad was the treasurer of the pre-eternal expressions of grace, Eblis was that of the post-eternal expressions of wrath. God created Moḥammad from the light of grace and Eblis from the fire of wrath. The subtle one [Moḥammad] produced expressions of grace, while the coarse one [Eblis] produced those of wrath. It is said these two were attributes of God, 'the Gracious' and 'the Wrathful'. "He leads astray whom He wills and He guides aright whom He wills." (XVI:93)

SS 510

God brought Moḥammad to the site of vision *(shohud)* revealing Himself to Eblis from 'the Eternal', showing Himself through the brides of the angelic realm (*malakut*) and helping him to view the realm of divine power (*jabarut*). The eye of the Prophet was not distracted from God by God's action. He plunged into the sea of the awesomeness of 'the Essence'. He observed the deception inherent in 'the Eternity' and took refuge from it in God, separating himself from the creation. He sought help from 'the Eternal Being', saying "I seek refuge in You from You."

God brought Eblis to the site of the pre-eternal state of wrath. Such that he saw God in the garb of wrath. Eblis threw himself into the wrath of God and became wrath itself. His gnosis increased through vision of wrath and he became intimate with wrath. God tested him through the hidden nature of divine deception, displaying the eternal form of Adam without the eternal spirit, saying, "Prostrate yourself before Adam!" Eblis was obsessed with the vision of divine wrath.

Through God's will Eblis became absent from God, because God subtlely disguised himself in Adam through his mysterious actions and his luminous attributes such that Eblis could not recognise God, nor could he recognise that Adam was God's creature. Eblis remained too pre-occupied with witnessing God's wrath and saw himself and imagined himself as clothed with the 'Divine Being'. Concentrating upon himself he became proud of the fact that he was decked out with the actions, knowledge and vision of God's wrath imagining that all of this was God; yet it was not God; it was only Eblis. Eblis was the servant, and Adam was God himself whom Eblis failed to see because of his pride. Throwing off the rope of devotion he said, "I am better than him [Adam]." In fact he had seen nothing better, he had seen no superior goodness in himself but had merely assumed it through analogy. But how can one use analogy in relation to God and His creation? If Eblis had seen those qualities in Adam which the other angels had seen, the effulgence of Adam's soul would have melted Eblis with 'eternal' light immediately. Adam at that point was illumined with 'eternal' light and the glory of the Divine Essence and attributes. Since Eblis 'the accursed one' didn't see Adam, he claimed superiority over Adam. Eblis returned to his former condition falling from the 'the eye of God' (*'ain-e ḥaqq*), to become 'that stranger to the world' as [*Ḥallâj*] had indicated.

SS 511

'Aino'l-Qoḍhât Hamadâni said, "Put aside 'jealousy-in-love' (*ghairat*)[1], O dear friend! Don't you know what that maddened lover, whom you called 'Eblis' in this world, was called in the divine world? If you knew his name, you would consider yourself an unbeliever in calling him by that name. Take care in what you hear! That crazy one loved God. Do you know what occurred by way of a test of loving-kindness? On the one hand, affliction and wrath; on the other blame and humiliation. He was told that if he claimed to love God, he should prove it. The tests of affliction and wrath and of blame and humiliation were presented to him, and he accepted them.

1. *Ghairat* is the determined attention of the lover's heart to keep the Beloved from being attached to anyone else, and to keep himself from being attached to anything other than this Beloved.

At that time these tests proved that his love was true. You have no idea what I am talking about! In love there must be both rejection (*jafâ'*) and acceptance (*wafâ'*), so that the lover may become mature through the grace and wrath of the Beloved; if not he remains immature and unproductive.

Be aware that perfection in love is one of the stations of love, in that if one is vilified by the Beloved, one is happier than if one had received grace from others. One who does not know this, is ignorant in the way of love. Be aware that once you have turned these words over in your mind and reflected upon them, you may conclude that God's friends are cultivated by his grace and wrath. They grow drunk a thousand times a day from the wine of union and are ultimately crushed by separation from the Beloved. The lover is still a disciple, and in this world disciples are hung from the tree of separation...

A thousand times a day the inner being of the seeker of the divine presence answers, 'We know that our Beloved comes with wrath and affliction, but we have pledged ourselves to the Beloved's affliction and wrath. From the Beloved comes affliction and from us contentment, from the Beloved, wrath, from us love'...

What a love it is that cries, 'We have chosen eternal pain, consigning mercy and grace to others!'... O friend, do you know where Eblis' pain comes from? First he was the treasurer of heaven, one of the seraphim; from that station, he descended to the station of the world and was appointed treasurer of the world and hell.

Are you aware of what he said? He said, 'For several thousand years I resided in the way of the Beloved. When the Beloved accepted me, my portion was His rejection.' Then what do you suppose Eblis said? He said, 'When mercy befell me, the Beloved cursed me saying, "And My curse be upon you till the Day of Judgement!"' (XXXVIII:78)... What would you say of someone, who, being deprived of nourishment, continued to live on and thrive? ...By the Divine Grandeur, unless God tells Eblis to do something, he will not do it.

If you knew that 'Nor doth he speak of [his own] desire,' (LIII:3) concerns Moḥammad, you may then be aware that (notwithstanding that Eblis was doing the same thing as

Moḥammad, namely that he spoke when directed to do so by God), 'In their story there is indeed a lesson for those of understanding.' (XII:3) One of the lessons provided is this, that Benjamin, and all those who were privy to the secret, knew that he had not committed a theft (XII:70-83); yet Joseph told him to publicly admit to having done so.

Be aware that where Gabriel, Michael and the other angels heard, 'Prostrate yourself before Adam,' God said to Eblis, in the innermost secretness of the visible and invisible realms, 'Prostrate only before Me!' Outwardly he told Eblis, '... Prostrate yourself before Adam...' (XVII:61), while inwardly he said, 'O Eblis, ask, "Should I prostrate before one whom you have created from clay?" ' (XVII:61) This is a different matter altogether.

Did you know that God has two names? One 'the Merciful, the Compassionate' (*ar-Raḥmâno'r-Raḥim*) and the other, 'the Almighty, the Proud' (*al-Jabbaro'l-Mostakber*). From the attribute of 'almightiness' he brought Eblis into being, and from that of 'mercifulness', he brought Moḥammad into being. Thus, the attribute of 'wrath' nurtures Eblis, while that of 'mercy' nurtures Moḥammad.

'O friend,' God said to Eblis, 'My curse be upon you till the Day of Judgement' (*din*, literally, 'religion'). By this, God did not mean the religion of this world, but the religion of the next. That religion is self-effacement and oneness of the religious community. In this world such religion is called infidelity. What is infidelity? What is faith? Both are one.

Not everyone can fathom that both Eblis and Moḥammad claim to be guides on the Path. Eblis guides one away from God, while Moḥammad guides one towards God. God appointed Eblis the gatekeeper of His court, saying to him, 'My lover, because of the jealousy-in-love that you have for me, do not let strangers approach me.'

Alas! Eblis' sin was his love of God. Do you know what the sin of Moḥammad was? It was God's love for him. That is to say, while Eblis' falling in love with God was his sin, God's falling in love with Moḥammad was Moḥammad's sin, as is demonstrated in the passage, 'May God forgive you [Moḥammad] for your sin, that which has passed and that which is to come..." (XLVIII:2) One would need an entire world in order to portion out but a tiny atom of this sin. This represents the trust (*amânat*) bestowed upon Moḥammad, and those of Adam's nature. In spite of all this, God said, '[Adam] has proved a tyrant and a fool.'[1] Although the whole world denied even a tiny atom of this sin, the entirety of it was placed on the spirit of Moḥammad.

The pardon for this sin is automatic for one, as indicated by the verse, 'May God forgive you for your sin, that which has passed and that which is to come...' (XLVIII:2)

T 221-9

'Aṭṭâr praises Eblis in the following verses:

When Shebli's love became enflamed they tied him down in bonds by force.

A group went to him suddenly, and stood before him, looking at him.

The eloquent Shebli asked them, "Tell me then, who are you?"

"Why," they said, "we are friends, we know only friendship for you."

As soon as he heard these words from the friends, Shebli started to throw stones at them.

When the stones struck his visitors they jumped up to run away.

Shebli said, "Now then, you liars and lost ones,

When you boasted of your friendship with me, you were not being honest, ignoble ones.

Who would run away from wounding by a friend, for a wound that's inflicted by a friend is mercy;

Eblis did not flee when wounded by the Friend; but from that wound fashioned a hundred cures.

1. (XXXIII:72) "Indeed We offered the trust to the heavens and the earth and the mountains, and they refused to bear it, being afraid of it, while man assumed it. Indeed, he has proved oppressive and ignorant."

Accept in the soul every wound that the Friend inflicts, for if he strikes a wound in the soul, he strikes it well.

If an atom of love should appear, you will buy that wound with all your soul.

Do not suppose that his wounding is gratis; its price is thousands of years of devotion.

Although Eblis was devoted for thousands of years, his reward was one hour of cursing from God.

The proof that you are firmly in God's favour is that he denies that you are worthy of him.

Hear the story of Eblis, dear one; be honest for a while and listen.

If for a while, you were a man like Eblis, from you, at every moment, a new world would be born.

Although Eblis is cursed and repelled, he is still in the King's presence.

Why keep cursing Eblis night and day? From him learn 'Moslem-ness' just this once!"

EN 137

Rumi, in his *Mathnawi,* portrays Eblis as saying:

Even in affliction I take pleasure in him; I'm transfixed by him, transfixed by him, transfixed by him.

How can anyone liberate himself from this material world when he is bound by it?

How can anyone who is a part of this world be freed from its totality? Especially when God has created him imperfect.

Whoever is in the world is plunged in a fire; his liberator has to be the Creator of this world.

Whether faith or unbelief, they are both created by and come from God.

MM II 2647-51

Certain Sufis have maintained that because Eblis was in love with God, his jealousy-in-love did not want his Beloved to belong to anyone but him; and this is why he refused to prostrate before Adam. Eblis' jealousy-in-love has incurred the envy of certain of the great Sufis, a subject on which Sufi masters have remarked, as follows:

> To keep the unworthy from going too far, God made 'Azâzil from his tresses, then placed him before his door as his chamberlain.

Sabzawâri

The lover becomes jealous-in-love when his Beloved bestows affection on someone else. Eblis' jealousy-in-love was aroused when others bestowed their affections on his Beloved. The angels had the same jealousy-in-love as Eblis toward Adam, but with respect to Adam's love for God, and they said, "What right did Adam, who was from the earth, have to claim love for the Lord of Lords?

RSh III 234

> You have heard that one of the great ones posed this question to wandering Eblis.
> "Why did you not prostrate to Adam, when God commanded you to do so?"
> Eblis answered, "Once, a Sufi was on his way to a house.
> The daughter of the Sultan of that time, a beauty and a heart-breaker,
> Was being carried in a golden litter. Suddenly a breeze blew open the curtains of the litter.
> The Sufi's eye fell upon her beauty; a fire kindled within his being.
> The girl became aware of him, and called him to her, by the litter.

'O Sufi,' she said, 'why have you become so confused? What has happened that you are so distressed?'

The Sufi said, 'The Sufi has nothing but heart; the problem is, you've stolen that heart.'

The girl then said, 'Don't talk like that; you should not seek union with me;

If you were to see my sister but once, the arrow of her lashes would bend your back like a bow.

If you do not believe me, take a look; she's coming behind me right now.'

The fickle Sufi looked behind her, and the girl flung down the curtain of her litter.

'If he had but a grain of love,' she said, 'he would never have been attracted by anyone else.'

She summoned a servant and said, 'Quick, seize this Sufi and cut off his head,

So that no one in love with a beauty like me will ever let his eyes wander to another.' "

This story sheds light on the story of Eblis, I know no one who doubts this.

'Aṭṭâr MN 242-4

On his deathbed, Shebli was disturbed; he closed his eyes with a restless heart.

He bound the cincture of perplexity about himself and sat upon a heap of ashes.

Sometimes a tear would mingle with the ashes; sometimes he would sprinkle those ashes on his head.

"Have you ever seen," a person asked, "someone so distressed at such a time?"

"I am burning," Shebli replied, "What can I do? I am dissolving in jealousy-in-love, what can I do?

Because my soul has stitched its eye from both worlds, it burns with jealousy of Eblis' jealousy-in-love at this time.

Since God has reserved his curse for Eblis, I envy him; I am burning with expectation, but God has provided for another."

If you distinguish between a gem and a stone received from the King, you are not a man of the path!

If you're pleased with a gem and disappointed by a stone, you have no interest, then, in the King.

Neither like the gem, nor dislike the stone; consider only that both are from the hand of the King.

If the drunken Beloved throws a stone at you, it is better than receiving a gem from another.

It takes a man to seek God, to be always ready to sacrifice his soul upon the path. Never should one cease to seek.

Never should there be a moment's rest, for, if but for a moment one wavers in seeking, one will depart, with grace, from this Path of love.

'Aṭṭâr MT 183

HIGH ASPIRATION IN LOVE

Eblis' aspiration in love was so high that he considered the curse of the Beloved to be the expression of the perfect majesty of the Beloved, because the aspiration (*hemmat*) of love creates the desire for the Beloved to be majestic.

Aḥmad Ghazâli writes concerning this: Love possesses such aspiration that it makes one desire that the Beloved be majestic. Hence, the lovers aspiration is not content with just any beloved that may fall into his snare. It was with regard to this that God said to Eblis, "Indeed, My curse is upon you till the Day of Judgement" (XXXVIII:78). Eblis replied "Then by Your majesty..." (XXXVIII:82), meaning: "I myself love this majesty of Yours, of which no one is worthy or deserving, for if anyone were, You would not be perfect in Your majesty."

S 55

The Sufis consider Eblis to be amongst the *javânmardân*[1]. He did not prostrate before Adam because in the realm of chivalry (*fotowwat*) one should not honour another above one's friend. In observing this chivalry, Eblis displayed such manliness that he accepted the curse of pre-eternity and post-eternity, but was not prepared to let his name be stricken from the register of the *javânmardân* by prostrating before Adam.

Hallâj said, "I conversed with Eblis and Pharaoh on the subject of chivalry. Eblis maintained that if he had bowed before Adam, he would have been stricken from the register of the *javânmardân.* Pharaoh said that if he had believed in God's prophet [Moses], he too, would have been stricken from that register.

"I maintained that if I were to disavow my own claim, my own declaration ['I am God'], I also would be removed from the ranks of the *javânmardân.*"

TH 50

What a *javânmard!* Manṣur Ḥallâj said, "Only Moḥammad and Eblis practised chivalry." Truly, what do you understand of these words of Ḥallâj? He said that chivalry was properly observed by only two persons, Moḥammad and Eblis. These two achieved chivalry and valour. The rest are no more than children on the path. The *javânmard* Eblis said, "If others run from a slap [from God], I welcome it."

He said, "Since this keepsake was given to me by my Beloved, I don't care if it be good or bad, and anyone who distinguishes between the two is still immature in love. From the hand of the Friend it matters not whether it be honey or poison, sweet or sour, grace or wrath. One who is in love with the grace alone, is in love with himself, not with the Beloved. When the King bestows his own special cloak and cap on the lover nothing else matters to him."

1. *Javânmardân* are those people who dedicate their being and everything they possess to their friend, or indeed to anyone, expecting nothing in return.

When Eblis was asked why he did not fling the black mantle of 'My curse' from his shoulder, he replied:

I'll not sell the mantle, no never!
If I were to sell it, I would be naked.

TT 223

PRIDE IN LOVE

Certain Sufi masters maintain that Eblis was displaying such pride in love, that he refused to acknowledge what was other than God, when, in answering the Beloved's command, "Prostrate before Adam," he said, "You created me of fire and you created him of clay." (VII:12) With the closeness that Eblis had, it would have been inappropriate for him to have said, "I am God," like Manṣur Ḥallâj.

In reality, grace and wrath complement each other, such that, given the kind of wrath which God gave to Eblis, he conferred a perfection upon him which was worthy of pride.

Do you know what is meant by the 'cheek' and 'mole' of the Beloved? Has the black light above the Throne not been explained to you? It is the light of Eblis, which has been likened to the tresses of God; compared with the Divine Light it is darkness, but it is light just the same.

Do you know what the black light is? It is the cloak of "...and he became an unbeliever." (II:34) He has drawn the sword of "Then by Your Majesty, I will surely lead them all astray." (XXXVIII:82) Having entered the realm of darkness "...amid the darkness of land and sea," (XXXVII:63) he has lost control of himself. He has been made the guardian of truth. He has become the gatekeeper of that 'Majestic One' who said, "I take refuge in God from the accursed Satan."

Without question, one who sees the Beloved [as Eblis did] with such a 'curl', 'mole', 'tress' and 'eyebrow', will declare, like Ḥallâj, "I am God".

Some people who are at every moment in the tavern of ruin of "And God inspired it [man's soul] with [a conscience of] what is wrong for it," (XCI:8), are given the potion of wrath and unbelief, while some people who are in the state of "I am the city of knowledge and 'Ali is its gate,"[1] are given the potion of "I was the guest of my Lord last night," this being the state of the pious. Both potions are constantly being provided and both groups are forever seeking more. God's drunken ones, who are in the Ka'ba of being "firmly established in the favour of a Mighty King," (LIV:55) are made drunk by "their Lord [dispensing] to them pure wine." (LXXVI:21) Another group who are in the tavern of ruin of "And God inspired it..." act insanely. After all, has the one who "whispers in the breasts of mankind" (CXIV:5), never battled with you?

People have only heard the name of Eblis and do not know that he possessed such pride in love that he acknowledged no one! Do you know why he had this pride? It is because the light of Eblis [the tresses] is close to the cheek and mole [the light of Moḥammad]. Can the cheek and the mole ever be complete without the tresses, eyebrow and hair? By God, they are not complete! Do you not see that in the daily prayer (*namâz*) one is required to say, "I take refuge in God from the accursed Satan?" This is why he is proud and practises, coyness and coquetry, for he is the chief of the arrogant and selfish. "You created me out of fire and You created him out of clay," (VII:12), is the very expression of that pride in love.

If you do not believe this, then hear the word of God: "Praise be to God, who has created the heavens and the earth and has established darkness and light." (VI:1) How can black be complete without white or white without black be complete? It cannot be. The Divine Wisdom has so ordained. The Wise One *(al-Ḥakim)*[2], according to His wisdom, considered it must be so, and it is fitting to be so. Everything functions by design in God's court, and if the slightest imperfection were to be found in the creation, it would mean imperfection in the Wise One and his wisdom. Beings and creatures are created and graced in the [divine] lights.

1. See the author's *Traditions of the Prophet*, Vol.I. p.45.
2. One of the Names of God.

O dear one, listen to what a great one has said about these two stations: "Indeed, faith and unbelief have become two veils beyond the Divine Throne[2], separating God from the devotee," for a man must be neither unbeliever nor Moslem. If he is still involved with either faith or unbelief, he is still involved with these two veils. The advanced wayfarer is involved only with the veil of the splendour of the Essence of God.

T 118-123

SELF-SACRIFICE

Certain Sufi masters have maintained that Eblis was the paragon of lovers in self-sacrifice because he was not prepared to prostrate before other than the Beloved, and accepted the eternal curse wholeheartedly. This is illustrated by 'Aṭṭâr as follows:

First, go and become a man of the Path, like the manly ones; then sacrifice your soul before the King.
Eblis is never for a moment free of his burning; learn the lesson of manliness from the accursed Eblis.
He emerged as a man on the field of claims; everything about him was made worthy by God.

EN 105

Ghazâli said, "Though Satan was cursed and humiliated, he was still the paragon of lovers in self-sacrifice."

MAG 79

1. This is the realm of the qualities of God, and is to be distinguished from God's Essence.

Ḥallâj recounted that his masters and teachers were Eblis and Pharaoh. Eblis was threatened with fire; yet he did not retract his position. Pharoah was drowned in the sea; yet he did not disavow his claim. Neither of them accepted any intermediaries.

TH 51

According to Ruzbehân: In the 'beginning' Eblis fell into the sea of gnosis, understanding what he could of Reality. Through God Himself, he became proud before God. Then the ocean of divine unity cast him on the shore of isolation. Yet despite his outward refusal to acknowledge [Adam], he remained collected in the Divine Presence. This refusal beguiled him into abandoning all intermediaries, saying that intermediaries are a form of partnership (*sherk*) with God with respect to the isolation of Divine Unity. As he was in the state of concentration, he became immune to dispersion and could afford to disobey [God's command to prostrate]. He rejected dispersion, refusing to refer the primary to the secondary. Eblis' inner consciousness (*serr*) deceived him, telling him not to turn away from the Eternal Beloved to the non-existent Beloved [Adam], and this deceit brought him serenity. He did not understand the nature of the deceit, because in eternity there is no non-existence. He did not know that the reality of dispersion is concentration, nor that there is no 'Adam' but God. He was in error, remaining veiled from unity by having seen it.

SS 376

1. Intermediaries (*wasâ'eṭ*): the means employed to reach one's end.

Certain of the Sufi masters have refrained from condemning Eblis, some even going as far as to hold him in the highest esteem, as the following passage from 'Aino'l-Qoḍhât Hamadâni demonstrates:

O man of honour! If "And God spoke directly to Moses," (IV:164), signifies perfection, then Eblis enjoys such perfection. How do you know who Eblis really is? Eblis' station is closed to you. If you were to attain it, you would see that the motto above his door reads thus:

O my Beloved, I bear your suffering and I fight for you;
I do not mix your love with that of another.
I have a soul which bears the burden of your love;
I shall not give up until it is satisfied in your way.

'Aino'l-Qoḍhât goes on to quote the words of Aḥmad Ghazâli, who said, "I never heard Shaikh Abo'l-Ḥasan Kharaqâni say the name of Eblis without adding, 'That greatest of the great' and 'That paragon of the separated ones'. When I mentioned this to Baraka,[1] he told me that the title, 'Paragon of the Separated One's' is better than the Greatest of the Great'.

NAQ I 96-7

Ḥasan Baṣri honours Eblis in the following manner; Indeed, the light of Eblis is of the fire of the Magnificence, as in the words of God, "You created me of fire." (VII:12) And if Eblis were to reveal his light ot mankind, they would worship it like a God.

T 211

According to Abo'l-'Abbâs Qaṣṣâb, Eblis was slain by God. It would be unmanly to stone one who is slain by God. If God were to place the reckoning of the Day of Judgement in

1. A Sufi Shaikh contemporary with 'Aino'l Qoḍhât.

my hands, this is what I would do: I would assemble everyone and give Eblis a high station before them, but God would not place the reckoning in my hands.

TA 643

It is recounted that Nuri and another man were sitting together, both weeping piteously. When the other left, Nuri turned to his companions and asked, "Did you know who this person was?" When they replied that they did not, he said, "It was Eblis, and he was telling me about his service, recounting all that had happened to him, moaning of the pain of separation, and crying as you saw; I too was moved to tears."

TA 470

Râbe'a was asked, "Do you love the Almighty?" She replied, "Yes I do." Then they asked, "Are you the enemy of Satan?" She replied, "I am so involved in the Merciful that I have no time for hostility towards Satan."

TA 80

NOT LOOKING UPON EBLIS WITH CONTEMPT

Rumi illustrates the danger of scorning Eblis in the following passage from the *Mathnawi:*

> One day Adam looked upon Eblis the heartless, with contempt and with scorn.
>
> He behaved with conceit and favoured himself; he laughed at the plight of the accursed Eblis.
>
> God, out of jealousy-in-love, cried out, "O chosen one! You are ignorant of the hidden mysteries.
>
> If God wished, he could tear up the mountain, root and base; he could shame a hundred Adams and bring forth a hundred Eblises as new converts to Islam."
>
> "I repent from this attitude," cried Adam, "I will not be so disrespectful again."

O help of those who call for succour'[1] guide us!
There is no pride in knowledge or in riches.

Do not let stray that heart which you have guided with benevolence, and turn aside the evil which your Pen has prescribed.

Let the ill that's foreordained pass from our souls and do not cut us off from the brethren of contentment.[2]

Nothing is more bitter than separation from you; without your protection there's nothing but perplexity.

MM I 3893-3902

THE MANIFESTATION OF THE DIVINE NAME, 'THE MISGUIDER' *(al-moḍhell)*

Eblis is the manifestation of the divine name, 'the Misguider', which is contained in the divine name, 'Allâh', of which man is the all-inclusive manifestation. For this reason it has been said that every human being has a Satan within. Thus, the Prophet said, "My Satan was made Moslem by me." The fact of the matter is that Satan is within, having no external existence at all, as the following poem by Sabzawâri confirms:

The unveiling of the Majesty caused the manifestation of Wrath;
How then have these dualists created Satan everywhere?

Some maintain that the Prophet of God is the manifestation of the Name, 'the Guide' (*al-hâdi*) and that Eblis is that of 'the Misguider', while God is the manifestation, of both. Hence, Moḥammad enjoys the role of the guide and Eblis that of the misguider. This dichotomy is explained by Jâmi in the following verses:

God has two functions and names, each having many manifestations.

1. Reference to one of the Names of God.
2. The friends of God, those in whom He is well pleased.

They function in opposition to one another, one promoting unbelief, the other religion.

These two names are 'Guide' and 'Misguider'; I am revealing the reality of the matter.

The Prophet and his following manifest the former; Eblis and his following manifest the latter.

The former guides to truthfulness and rectitude, the latter to unbelief and veiling.

The former directs you to closeness, to nearness; the latter drives you to separation and darkness.

HA 79

CRITICISMS OF EBLIS

HARDHEARTED AND REJECTED FROM THE BEGINNING

Originally, Eblis was called 'Azâzil because it was preordained that he would be dismissed (*ma'zul*) from his place. He did not progress on the Path to God because he was hardhearted from the beginning.

TH 54, SS 529

SEEKING FAME CAUSES EBLIS' DISGRACE

Rumi illustrates Eblis' search for fame in the following verses:

> For years Eblis was renowned; then was disgraced; now how is he seen?
> In the world his stature was famed; his fame changed to infamy; alas for him!
> Till you are secure [in God] do not seek fame, wash your face of fear; then show your face.

MM II 8040-2

DISCOURTESY AND DISRESPECT

Certain of the Sufi masters believe that Eblis' sin was that of discourtesy and disrespect, because when God commanded him to prostrate before Adam, the etiquette of a lover demanded that he neither say "I" nor enter into dispute. The lover's manifestation of existence before the Beloved is an unpardonable sin, and the punishment for such misbehaviour and lack of respect was, for him, to be expelled from the court of the Beloved forever, as Rumi confirms in the following verses:

> Whoever behaves carelessly in the path of the Friend, is a highwayman who holds up men, and is, himself, no man.
>
> Through etiquette these heavens have become filled with light, and through etiquette the angels have become immaculate and pure.
>
> Through insolence the sun was eclipsed; through impudence 'Azâzil was turned from the door.

MM I 90-92

ATTENTION TO ADAM'S FORM WHILE UNAWARE OF ITS SPIRITUAL REALITY

Certain Sufi masters ascribe the cause of Eblis' disobedience to his consideration of the outward form (*ṣurat*) of Adam and his lack of awareness of the latter's inner reality (*ma'nâ*), which was the manifestation of the whole of the names and attributes of God. It was through this heedlessness and his refusal to prostrate before Adam, that he went astray.

Alluding to this Rumi writes:

> You have seen what Eblis the accursed has seen, when he said "I am of fire, while Adam is clay."
>
> Cover up the Eblis-like eye for just a moment; how long will you see just the form? How long, indeed, how long?

MM III 2299-30

Alas for that eye that's blind and bruised! Within it the sun seemed like an atom
Of an Adam who had no like. He saw nothing but a lump of clay.

MM III 2758-9

According to Ebn 'Arabi:
If Eblis had observed
the light through which Adam lived,
He would not have refused that prostration.

Tarjomân al-ashwâq 28

CONSIDERING HIMSELF SUPERIOR TO ADAM

In his *Ṭawâsin,* Ḥallâj relates that Eblis said to God, "Adam is neither dearer than me nor greater, for I knew you first in pre-eternity. I am better than him, because I have served you longer. There is no one in the world who knows you better than I. Your devotion works within me, and has done so from earliest time, as has my devotion to you. How could I prostrate myself before other than you? Because I didn't prostrate, I had no choice but to return to my original substance. You created me of fire, and fire returns to fire. Destiny and prerogative are yours."

TH 41

The same theme of Eblis' superiority can be found in the following verses of Rumi:

There is no worse disease in your soul, O coy one, than thinking you are perfect.
Much blood must flow from your heart and eye, till this conceit leaves you.
The failing of Eblis was "I am better than him," and this infirmity is in every creature's soul.
Though one may consider one's 'self' duly broken, know it's a stream of clear water with dung below.

When God's order makes you upset, your water turns to a crown of dung.

There's dung in the bed of the stream, my boy, though the stream may seem clear to you.

The master of the Path, full of understanding digs up the streams of both the 'self' and the body.

MM I 3214-20

When God commanded, "Prostrate before Adam," Eblis said, "How can I prostrate before Adam when you created me of fire and him of clay? The two are opposites of one another, being in no way harmonious; I have served you longer; I am of greater virtue and learning and my life is richer and longer."

TH 52

A hundred thousand years ago this very drunkenness-of-being waylaid Eblis.

From this drunkeness 'Azâzil became Eblis, saying, "Why should Adam dominate me?

I am noble, and also I am nobly born; I am capable, ready for a hundred virtues.

In virtue I am second to none; I do not stand before my enemy in service.

I'm born of fire, and he of mud; what is mud's place next to that of fire?

Where was he when I was leader of the world, the glory of the time?"

Rumi MM V 1921-6

Ḥallâj relates in his *Ṭawâsin* that Eblis knew more about prostration than all those who prostrated. He was nearest to God, readiest in the expenditure of all his forces and power, the most faithful in observance of oaths and closest to the presence of 'the Worshipped One'.

The others prostrated before Adam in accordance with God's command, while Eblis refrained, refusing because he had spent so long in contemplative vision and presence.

Thus he became distressed and confused, his thoughts became impure, and he said, "I am better than him," so that he remained veiled and disgraced, and was condemned to eternal punishment.

TH 55

IN A STATE OF INTOXICATION EBLIS SAID "I AM BETTER THAN ADAM"

Ruzbehân commented that the station of superiority is one in which the gnostic, being in a state of gnosis, knows himself as a friend of God, and he sees the focusing of the lights of the subtletics of God intensifying upon him. His state of union is unaffected by human qualities. By the light of sagacity he sees the degrees of creation through his nearness to God. The intoxication *(sokr)* of expansion *(baṣt)* and gladness *(enbesaṭ)* overcomes him, so that he does not care if he claims, "I am better than so-and-so," or "so-and-so will never attain my station." This kind of claim is characteristic of the intoxicated, and does not grace the one who claims it, as when Eblis said, "I am better than him [Adam]," and this station is disapproved of by the perfected ones.

There is no problem when one who is truly in love makes a declaration out of jealousy-in-love and fervour. After all, note what the best of God's creation, Mohammad, said, "I am the highest of the children of Adam, but I do not regard it as a distinction."

The gnostic [Ḥallâj] said, "Superiority means acceptance of God through the attributes of contentment *(reḍhâ)*[1] and subsistence *(baqâ)*[2] in union."

MA 185-6

1. For further discussion of *reḍhâ* see the author's *Sufism III* (London, 1985).
2. For further discussion of *sokr, basṭ,* and *baqâ,* see the author's *Sufism: Fear and Hope...* (New York, 1982).

THE JUSTIFICATION OF ADAM'S SUPERIORITY TO EBLIS

Certain of the Sufi masters have compared Eblis with Adam, suggesting reasons for the latter's superiority over the former, a few of which we present below.

* * *

Eblis is the manifestation of the Name, 'the Misguider' which is included in the all-embracing name [Allâh], while Adam is the manifestation of the all-embracing name itself.

RSh VI 378

Adam was nobler than Eblis in that the latter was of fire while Adam was of earth. Earth is better than fire, for fire reveals defect, while earth covers it. Whatever you give to fire, its defect is revealed. Real silver is distinguished from counterfeit. Gold alloy is distinguished from pure gold. Earth, on the other hand, covers defects. Whatever you put in the earth, earth covers it and its defects. Furthermore, fire causes disintegration, while earth produces union. Through fire comes cutting off and killing, whereas through earth comes joining and preserving. Eblis was of fire; hence he became separated. Adam was of earth, so he was joined [to God]. Moreover, the nature of fire is pride, the seeking of superiority, whereas the nature of earth is humility, the desiring of inferiority.

KAM III 49

Both Adam and Eblis ignored what they were commanded; however, there was a difference between them. Adam's sin stemmed from lust; Eblis' sin stemmed from pride. Proud behaviour is more severe than the acting out of lust. A sin which arises out of lust is pardonable, whereas that which arises from pride destroys one's faith.

KAM III 587

Adam's lapse was temporary; as a result he repented immediately.

Because Eblis' sin was essential; there was no way for him to precious penitence.

Rumi MM IV 3914-5

It has been said that Eblis deserved cursing and separation from the sanctuary of the 'Self-sufficient' on five counts, while Adam, in contrast, earned the mercy of God, the light of his guidance and the acceptance of his repentance in five respects:

1. Eblis did not admit to his sin. His pride did not permit him to do so, whereas Adam repented by virtue of his helplessness, and confessed to his sin. Rumi demonstrates this point in this verse:

Adam's lapse arose from the belly and sex; that of Eblis from pride and rank.

Hence, the former sought pardon straightaway, while the cursed one was too proud to repent.[1]

2. Eblis had no remorse for what he had done, nor did he seek forgiveness. Adam had remorse, sought pardon and made entreaty.

3. Eblis did not consider himself to be at fault in his disobedience and did not blame himself. Adam, on the other hand, assumed responsibility for his action and blamed himself for his lapse.

4. Eblis did not consider it necessary to repent; he did not seek pardon or make entreaty. Adam, however, knew that repentance is the key to felicity and the means to forgiveness; hence, he considered it necessary to repent, hastening to do so and not resting until his repentance was accepted.

5. Eblis lost hope in God's mercy. That unfortunate one did not know that despair is a quality of mean people and God is no mean person. Just as there is no despair within God, neither is there the need for assurance. Assurances belong to those who are helpless and God is not helpless. So, when 'the

1. MM V 520-1

evil one' despaired, the door of repentance was closed to him. Adam, however, did not despair, but fixed his heart upon God's mercy and forgiveness, weeping and lamenting on the divine threshold, until God's mercy and forgiveness were bestowed upon him.

KAM III 573

Shaikh Jonaid said that Eblis did not attain the direct vision of God *(moshâhadat)* in his devotion, whereas Adam's vision of God never faltered, even as he sinned. This means that devotion is obedience, which occurs outwardly, while 'vision' implies a sense of reverence, which occurs inwardly, for reverence arises from respect. So, for Eblis it was a matter of outward obedience but at the same time lack of inward reverence and respect. Adam, on the other hand, disregarded God's commands while in a state of expansion, yet retained inner reverence and respect. So, devotion with the abandonment of respect is fruitless, but unintentional sinning, while retaining respect, is not harmful.

KST 435

When Eblis was really Eblis, no one knew that he was Eblis, nor did he himself. He appeared to be a pious worshipper, devoting himself to service, washing his face with the water of acceptance. When his foot slipped, it became apparent that he was neither friend nor devotee. On the other hand, Adam was sincere; he was a friend, but the secret of his friendship was concealed by the blessings of God. When his foot slipped, it became apparent that he was both friend and devotee.

KAM X 329

Adam ascribed his error to himself, saying, "O Lord, I have wronged myself." (VII:23), while Eblis ascribed his sin to God, saying, "Lord, because You have misguided me..." (XV:39) As Rumi illustrates in the verses below:

Satan said, "Because You have misguided me...," the despicable devil covered up his act.

Adam said, "I have wronged myself"; he was not ignorant of God's action, unlike ourselves.

Out of etiquette, by accepting the responsibility for sinning, he concealed God's action; by taking the sin upon himself he was blessed.

After his repentance God asked him, "Did I not create the sin and those tribulations within you?

Was it not my ordainment and decree? Why then did you hide it when asking for forgiveness?"

"I was afraid," said Adam, "I preserved etiquette." God replied, "And I, in turn, have rewarded you for this."

MM 1488-93

ADAM AS THE TOUCHSTONE OF EBLIS THE DISGRACED

In Sufi writings Adam is sometimes alluded to as the touchstone by which Eblis was tested, after which Eblis emerged disgraced. Rumi illustrates this in the following verses:

You have laughed at Eblis and the devils, because you have seen yourself as virtuous.

When the soul turns its fleece coat inside-out, many a "Woe is me!" will it wring from the religious.

All goldsmiths smile behind their counters, for the touchstone is hidden out of sight.

Do not lift the veil from us, O Veiler; in testing us be our protector!

The counterfeit presents itself like gold at night; the true gold awaits the break of day.

When it speaks, the gold declares, "Wait, O forged one, till the day discloses all!"

For a hundred thousand years, cursed Eblis was *abdâl*[1] and prince of the believers.

He clashed with Adam out of pride and became disgraced like dung at dawn.

MM I 3290-7

USE OF INTELLECTUAL ANALYSIS IN RELATION TO GOD'S COMMAND

In the following story from the *Mathnawi*, Rumi attributes the cause of Eblis' expulsion by the Beloved to the use of intellectual analysis and analogy with regard to the divine command.

The first to present these petty arguments in the presence of the lights of God, was Eblis.

He said, "There is no doubt that fire is better than earth. I am from fire, while he is of the earth.

So, comparing the derivative with the fundamental, he is from darkness and I am from bright light."

"No," God said, "On the contrary, there shall be no such comparisons; asceticism and piety are the *mehrâb*[2] pointing towards grace.

This is not the heritage of the transient world, which you find through 'relation'; it is spiritual.

Rather this is the heritage of the prophets; the souls of the devout are the inheritors thereof.

The son of Abu Jahl[3] became a believer; the son of Noah, though, joined the ones who had gone astray.

The one born of earth became illumined like the moon; you are born of fire; go darkened and in disgrace!"

1. A category of *wali*-s or friends of God considered to be constant in number in the world at any given time. See the author's *Farhang-e Nurbakhsh* Vol VI, p.22 for further discussion of *abdâl*.
2. The niche in the mosque which indicates the direction of prayer.
3. An early enemy of the Prophet.

The wise man has used such analogies and enquiry for finding the *qebla*[1] on cloudy days or at night.

However, when the sun and Ka'ba are before your face, do not seek to reason with such analogy and enquiry.

MM I 3396-405

NOT ACKNOWLEDGING HIS ERROR CAUSES CONFLICT AND DISPUTATION WITH GOD

The Sufis have used Eblis as an example to show the dangers of not admitting one's faults and errors. The following passage from Rumi's *Mathnawi* illustrates Eblis' failure to acknowledge his error and the consequent conflict and dispute caused with God himself.

Consider yourself a sinner. Call yourself one; do not be afraid! In order that the teacher[2] might not steal the lesson from you.

When you say, "I am ignorant, teach me," this honesty is better than a [false] reputation;

Learn from your father,[3] O fortunate one; "O Our Lord," he said, "We have done wrong."

He neither made excuses nor made up falsehoods, nor did he hoist the banner of deception and evasion.

Eblis, however, argued, saying, "I was ruddy, you made me pale.

The colour is yours; you are the dyer; you are the root of my sin, bane and pain."

Read, "Lord, because you have misled me..."[4] Do not become a determinist [like Eblis].

1. The direction of Moslem prayer.
2. Eblis
3. Adam.
4. "Because you have misled me, I shall indeed adorn the path of error for them on the earth and shall misguide them all." (XV:39)

How long are you going to keep climbing the tree of determinism and leaving your free will aside,

Like that Eblis and his progeny in conflict and dispute with God?

MM IV 1387-405

You too, O lover, since your crime has been disclosed, don't try to cover it up; humble yourself.

Those who are the elect descendants of Adam breathe forth the fragrance of "We have done wrong."

Express your need; do not dispute like Eblis the accursed, the insolent.

If ever insolence concealed his faults, then persist in such insolence and strife.

MM IV 346-9

DISMISSING HIS OWN ERRORS, EBLIS ASKS GOD FOR LONG LIFE

In the following passage, using Eblis as an example, Rumi describes the value and benefits of repentance.

Like Eblis, the crow sought bodily life until Resurrection, from the immaculate unique God.

Eblis said, "Give me time till the Day of Judgement;"[2] He should have said, "We repent, our Lord."

Life without repentance is life with misery; absence from God is death in the present moment.

MM V 768-70

1. Reference to Koran VII:14, which reads, "He said 'Reprieve me till the Day of Judgement.' "

Contentiousness:

By disputing God's command, Eblis overstepped his limits, and this caused him to be separated from God.

God makes that argument of yours like a dragon,
so that, in answering, it tears you to pieces.
Eblis the cursed, disputed and he was cursed till the
Day of Judgement.

Rumi MM II 2791-2

Envy:

According to Rumi, Eblis lost his proximity to God, because he became envious of Adam.

If, on the path, envy seizes you by the throat, it is
Eblis, who was envious in the extreme.
His envy made him disdainful of Adam, and from
this envy he is at war with destiny.

MM I 429-30

Pride in Past Actions:

Ḥâtem Aṣamm said, "Be careful not to let your situation make you proud, for there was no better place than heaven, and Adam experienced it. And also, be not proud of your devotion; Eblis' experience taught him this."

RQ 196

Self-worship:

Certain Sufi masters attribute the cause of Eblis' separation from the station of nearness to God, to his self-worship; he said "I" before the command of God.

 As 'Aṭṭâr writes:

> God the most high spoke privately to Moses, saying, "Go forth and learn a secret from Eblis."
>
> As soon as he saw Eblis, Moses asked him to tell him a secret.
>
> "Keep this discourse always in mind," said Eblis, "Never say 'I', lest you end up like me.
>
> Even if you express the merest hint of existence, you are an unbeliever, not a devotee.
>
> Achievement on the path lies in the absence of fulfillment; the good man is one who has a bad reputation amongst people;
>
> Because if there should be fulfillment on the way, a hundred 'I's will appear all at once."
>
> MT 163

Lack of Friendship:

Certain Sufi masters believe that the reason for Eblis' separation was his lack of friendship with God. Though he had gnostic cognition, he did not have friendship.

* * *

Claiming friendship without knowledge is denial, while the claiming of knowledge without friendship is deceitful. Therefore Eblis, who was known as 'the rejected' and 'chief of villains', enjoyed knowledge but not friendship. Both his beginning and his end were the essence of deception, sunk in the depths of infidelity.

Outwardly he presented the form of an angel, wearing the mask of holiness, while his inner being was corrupt. He spent thousands of years treading the path of devotion in the hope of union; consequently, he expected his inner eye to be open or that the fragrance of union might permeate his inner being. He fell from the lofty heavens to the earth of accursedness.

KAM III 468

Destitution:

Man is in the prison of the world, so that he may realise his destitution.

Our God proclaimed in our Koran, the destitution of Eblis,

Warning of his trickery, destitution and evil counsel; do not join him or form any partnership with him.

And if you do so, using him as your excuse, he is destitute; how will you gain?

MM II 653-6

Deceitfulness:

Eblis appealed, "O Source of Peace! O Lord! Give me time till the Day of Resurrection.[1]

For I am content to be in the prison of this world, so that I may slay my enemy's offspring.

Those who have some victual of faith, or a loaf of provision to take on the way,

This I shall snatch by deception or fraud, so that in regret, they raise a hue and cry.

"Sometimes I may threaten them with destitution, or bind their eyes with tresses and with mole."

In this prison the victuals of faith are sparse, and what's there is hidden in the pot away from the eye of this cur.[3]

Prayer and fasting and a hundred helpless states provide him with the victuals of fervour.

I seek refuge in God from his Satan; we have perished alas, through his aggressiveness.

1. VII:14, XV:36, XXXVIII:79.
2. Consciousness of the world of multiplicity. See the author's *Sufi Symbolism* Vol.I, p.44 and 78-84.
3. Eblis, who is incited by that which is hidden from him.

One cur he is, yet he enters thousands; whomever he enters becomes just like him.

Whoever dampens your spirit, know that Satan is within him; the Devil's become hidden under his skin.

When he does not find form, he enters through the imagination, and that imagination leads you into misdoing;

It may be imagination of worldly success or of commerce, or of knowledge, or of house and home.

MM II 630-41

Bad Company:

Beware! Do not hearken to the blandishments of the bad companion; look out for the trap; do not walk upon the earth with over-confidence.

Behold the hundred thousand devils who are uttering, "There is no power and no force except in God." O Adam, see Eblis in the serpent!

He flatters you, calling you, 'Ah, my dearest friend', so that like a butcher, he may skin his friend.

He flatters you in order to skin you; too bad for the one whose antidote is administered by the foe.

He lays his head at your feet like the butcher[1] who wants to skin you like a sheep. Woe! Woe!

Like a lion, hunt your prey yourself; do not depend on stranger or kin.

MM II 256-61

Trickery:

Whoever associates with the unrighteous lowers himself and becomes stupid.

Be like a sword before strangers to God; don't play tricks like a fox; be a lion.

1. Once a butcher traditionally slaughters a sheep, he makes an incision in the skin of one of the legs and presses his lips to it, blowing into it, to separate the skin from the meat.

Then the friends of God will not break with you out of jealousy-in-love, for those thorns are foes of such roses.

Set those wolves on fire, like wild rue, for those wolves are foes of Joseph.

Eblis calls you, "My dear child"; watch out! He does it to deceive you, cursed devil!

He used the same tricks on your father, this disgraced one, to checkmate Adam.

He's sharp at chess, this crow; do not play with him with a drowsy eye,

Because he knows many brilliant moves which will catch in your throat like a splinter.

His splinter will stick in your throat for years; what is that splinter? Love of rank and wealth.

Possession is the splinter, O unstable one, while it's in your throat, it blocks the water of life.

If a clever enemy should snatch away your wealth, a highway robber will have carried off a highway robber![1]

MM II

Suspicion and Scepticism:

That suspicion and scepticism belongs to the hypocrite, who judges you from the standpoint of his own wicked soul.

When you put a piece of yellow-tinted glass before your eye, you see the sunlight coloured yellow.

Smash that yellow piece of glass, and distinguish the dust from the man.

The dust has swirled up around the horseman; you have imagined the dust to be the divine-man.

Eblis saw the dust and demanded to know how Adam, who was made from clay, was better than he who was made from fire.

1. Wealth itself is a highway robber.

As long as you see God's dear ones as ordinary, know that your view has been endowed by Eblis.

If you are not Eblis' offspring, O obstinate one, how has the inheritance of that cur come to you?

I [Rumi] am no cur; I am a lion of God, a worshipper of God; the lion of God is liberated from external form.

The lion of the world seeks prey and provision; the lion of the Lord seeks freedom and death.

Seeing, in death, a hundred existences, he burns away his being like the moth.

MM I 3957-66

CONSIDERING EBLIS AS THE CARNAL SOUL *(nafs)*

Certain Sufi masters have considered Eblis to be the carnal soul and its tendencies. They have seen the essence of Eblis as existing in human beings; Eblis enjoys no existence in his own right. It is this matter which we undertake to explain, by citing the following passages:

* * *

Every day the passions don three hundred and sixty styles of divine dress, inviting the wayfarer to go astray, but unless the passion for sinning manifests itself in one, Satan cannot penetrate the heart and inner being of the wayfarer. When the predisposition for the passion arises, Satan seizes and promotes it, projecting it upon the heart; this is what is known as 'temptation'; thus, it begins in passion, and this is the most vile of onslaughts. This is what is meant by God's answer to Eblis' declaration, "By Your might I shall misguide them all." (XXXVIII:82) God's reply was, "As for my bondsmen, you have no power over them, except for the erring one who follows you." (XV:42) So, in fact, Satan is no more than the wayfarer's carnal soul and passions. The Prophet was referring to this point when he said, "There is no one whom Satan has not dominated, except 'Omar, who has dominated his own Satan [his passions].

KM 262

The carnal soul and Satan have been one from the first,
And both have envied and been an enemy of Adam.

Rumi MM III 3197

The carnal soul and Satan exist as one,
Though they show themselves in two forms.

Rumi MM III 4053

One said to another, "Eblis out of pride comes to waylay me at the time of presence.[1]

Because I have not the strength to fight with him, anxiety befalls my heart at his deceit.

What can I do to be saved from him, and enjoy the wine of spiritual life?"

"As long as this cur of an ego is with you," his friend replied, "Eblis will not run from you very quickly.

Eblis' blandishments are based on your own dishonesty; each and every desire in you, is your Eblis.

If you should satisfy but one of your desires, a hundred more Eblises will be born within you.

This waste pit of a world, which is a prison, is the territory of Satan from end to end.

Try to keep your hands off his territory, so he will have nothing to do with you."

'Aṭṭâr MT

1. *Waqṭ-e hoḍhur.*

Sufis have recounted interesting and ironic anecdotes concerning Eblis in their works, two of which we present below:

One day, Solomon had a request to make, and said, "O Almighty God! You have placed jinn and man, bird and beast at my beck and call; how would it be if you were to subject Eblis also to my command, so that I might imprison him?" "O Solomon," God replied, "do not insist on this request; there is nothing to be gained from it." "Almighty God," entreated Solomon, "if you would but grant my request for just two days!" "It is done," said God. Solomon imprisoned Eblis. Now, with all the sovereignty at his disposal, Solomon still worked for his daily bread. Each day he wove a basket and sold it for two loaves of bread, which he ate with a poor man in the mosque, saying, "A poor man sits in the company of a poor man." The day he imprisoned Eblis, he sent the basket to the market but no one bought it, for there was no trading or commerce in the marketplace and everyone was engaged in prayer. That day Solomon did not eat. The next day he wove a basket as usual, and again no one bought it. Solomon grew hungry; he began to weep and appealed to God, "O Almighty God! I am hungry, for no one has bought a basket." "O Solomon," came the response, "do you not realise that, since you imprisoned the lord of the bazaar merchants, the door of trade is closed for humanity, and this is not good for the people!"

KAM VIII 360

Related by Sa'di in his *Bustan:*

A man was cheating people by misrepresentation; when he got up to go he cursed Eblis.
Meeting him, Eblis said to him, "I have never seen such a fool as you.
You and I are friends; why then do you pick a fight with me?"

‘AZIZO’D-DIN NASAFI CONCERNING EBLIS

EBLIS AS IMAGINATION (*wahm*) AND ADAM AS INTELLECT (*‘aql*) IN THE MACROCOSM

When God the Exalted brought creation into being, he called it ‘the world’ (*‘âlam*) in the sense that creatures are the signs (*‘alâmat*) of his existence, as well as the existence of his knowledge, will and power.

O darvish! On the one hand, creatures are a sign, and on the other they are a text. From the point of view of their being a sign, God called them ‘the world’, while from that of their being a text, he called them ‘the Book’. Then he said, “Whoever reads this book will come to know me, my knowledge, will and power.” At that time the readers were the angels, and the readers were few, while the Book was vast. The eyes of the readers were not able to reach to the corners of the pages of the Book. Because of this, God made a copy of this world and summarised the Book, calling the original ‘macrocosm’ and the copy ‘microcosm’. He designated the first as the Greater Book and the second as the Lesser Book. Now, whatever was in the Greater Book, he re-wrote in the Lesser Book without excess or defect, so that whoever might read this Lesser Book had in effect read the Greater. Thereupon God delegated his vicegerent to represent him in this microcosm, this divine vicegerent being the ‘intellect’. When the ‘intellect’ had taken up the vicegerency in this microcosm, all the angels of the microcosm prostrated before it, except 'imagination', which did not, refusing to bow, just as when Adam assumed the vicegerency in the macrocosm, all the angels prostrated to him, except Eblis, who did not.

EK (N) 143

SATAN AS NATURE AND EBLIS AS IMAGINATION

Six persons emerged from the third heaven: Adam, Eve, Satan, Eblis, the Peacock and the Snake.

Adam is the spirit, Eve the body, Satan nature, Eblis imagination, the Peacock lust, and the Snake wrath. When Adam approached the tree of intellect, he left the third heaven and entered the fourth. All the angels prostrated before Adam, except Eblis, who refused. That is to say, all the powers, spiritual and physical, became obeisant and obedient to the spirit, except imagination, which refrained from doing so.

EK (N) 301

AN EXPLANATION OF 'ANGEL', 'SATAN' AND 'EBLIS'

Know that the Shaikh of Shaikhs, Shaikh Sa'do'd-Din Ḥamawi said, "The angel is the unveiler and Satan the veiler," while the sovereign of lovers, 'Aino'l-Qoḍhât Hamadâni said, "The angel is the cause, and Satan the cause, as well, the angel being the cause of unveiling and Satan that of veiling. The cause of good is the angel, while that of evil is Satan. The cause of mercy is the Angel of Mercy, while that of torment is the Angel of Torment."

O darvish! Whoever invites you to good works and keeps you from evil ones, is your angel. Whoever invites you to evil deeds and keeps you from good ones is your Satan.

O Darvish! One night I saw the Prophet in the city of Nasaf, my home town. He asked, "O dear one, do you know who is the devil who recites 'I take refuge in God from the accursed Satan' and who is the Satan who recites, 'There is no power and no strength, save in God'?" "No, O Prophet of

God," I replied. The Prophet said, "So-and-So is the first and So-and-So is the second; stay clear of them". I knew both of them and had been associating with them. I stopped associating with them.

O Darvish! Adam who is the microcosm is a blend of both worlds, the material and the angelic. The material world is form and the angelic is spirit. The material world is body, and the angelic is soul. The material world is a house and the angelic is the lord of the house. There is a hierarchy of levels; in each level the lord of the house has a different name. At one level he is called 'nature'; at another 'carnal soul'; at another 'intellect'; and at another, 'the Light of God'.

Now that these levels have been introduced, know that nature, being the first level, brings three things into existence: the first, cultivation, development and obedience; the second, corruption, destruction and disobedience; and the third, pride, egotism and disobedience. For this reason the prophets have given nature three names. The one who cultivates, develops and obeys, is called 'angel'. The one who corrupts, destroys and disobeys, is called 'satan'. The one who is proud, egotistical and disobedient, is called 'Eblis'. In this context it has been said that every man has Satan as his companion, living with him. The Prophet said, "I have submitted Satan to my hand." So, the angel, Satan, and Eblis are one essence, and that sole essence has been ascribed various attributes and properties. Now, if one should call all three 'Satan', that would be correct, as well. "And the unruly, every builder and diver (made We subservient) [to Solomon], and others linked together in chains." (XXXVIII:37,38)

O Darvish! Now that you have learned the meaning of 'angel', 'Satan' and 'Eblis', know that amongst the common folk there is little knowledge thereof; amongst them are the angel and Satan. Eblis is amongst the wise men, the elders and the governors. It is they who are conceited and egotistical, being unable to consider anyone higher than themselves, hence, regarding all as having lower status.

EK (N) 403-5

THE MANIFESTATIONS, METHODS OF EBLIS

'Abdo'-l-Kerim ebn Ibrahim al-Jili in his *al-Ensân al-kâmel* has cited several manifestations of Eblis, which we shall set out here:

Know that Eblis appears in ninety-nine manifestations, equalling the number of the virtuous names of god, and he endlessly projects himself within these manifestations, the description of all of which would be difficult.

We shall confine ourselves to the seven manifestations which are fundamental, equivalent to the seven essential names of God, which are the basis for all the virtuous divine names. There is a wonder in this matter which is that Eblis' origin lies in the *nafs*[1] of the Divine Essence. Take note of this point and keep it ever in mind.

Now, know that the sevenfold manifestations are as follows:

The First Manifestation is the world and that which has been assigned to the world, such as the stars and the transcendent elements, as well as the natural elements. Now, take note that Eblis does not project his manifestation on any

1. The *nafs* of God (*an-nafs al-elâhiya)* has a particular meaning in Jili's terminology. It is intended to mean "the Divine Person, that is to say, God, insofar as He is endowed with the qualities such as Life, Will, Power, Word etc." See A Culme-Seymour's English translation of T. Burckhardt's *De l'Homme Universel* as *The Universal Man* (UK: Beshara Pub., 1983), p.XIX, 5, 43, 68.

particular person. However, he generally appears to each group in the manner which we shall describe. Furthermore, he is not content with the [effect of a] manifestation which he projects onto a given group; he persists in manifesting himself in different guises, until he has shut all doors of escape to them. All ways through which they may return to their original state are absolutely closed.

Here we shall discuss only the predominant manifestations displayed by Eblis to each group, leaving the rest aside, because Eblis achieves the same effect in all of his manifestations.

He appears to the idolators in the world, through the world and what exists in it, for example, the elements, the heavens and the transcendental elements, as well as the different climates of the world. He deceives the unbelievers and idolators with the collection of manifestations through the decoration and adornment of the world in the first instance, in order to destroy their reason and blind their hearts, whereupon he guides them through the mysteries of the stars and the principles of the elements and the like, telling them, "These things are the primary causes in existence." Consequently, they worship the heavens and become convinced of the correctness of his explanations of heavens. They witness how the sun fosters the material of existence with its heat and observe that the rain falls according to the findings of astronomy. Not a trace of doubt creeps into their conceptualising of the divine Lordship of the stars; when Eblis has established these principles amongst them, he makes them into four-legged creatures, whose efforts are directed solely towards feeding and watering themselves. They have no belief in the Day of Resurrection or anything like it; they kill and plunder one another, drown themselves in the seas of darkness of their natural appetites, and never find liberation therefrom.

Now, Eblis does the same for the believers in the elements, asking them, "Do you not see that matter is a composite of substances, which are in turn made up of heat and cold, moisture and dryness? These are your lords, they have brought forth existence and continue to be the primary causes in the world." Thus, Eblis does the same thing with this group that he has done with the first one.

He spoke similarly to the fire worshippers, asking, "Do you not see that 'being' has been divided into darkness and light, that darkness is a god called 'Ahriman' and light a god called 'Yazdân', and that the basis of fire is light?" Thereby they devotee themselves to the worship of that fire, so that he does the same thing with these as he has done with the first group and does likewise with all idolators.

The Second Manifestation is that of the desires of nature, lust and indulgence. Eblis appears to the ordinary Moslems in this manifestation in order to deceive them. First, he entices them into lustful pastimes, turning them towards animal indulgence [that which nature demands of them], so that the eye of insight for them becomes blind. At the same time he reveals the world to them, informing them that the desirable things which he reveals can be realised only through the world. Consequently, they become engulfed in love for the world, and persist in their attention to it. Having brought them to that stage, he leaves them to themselves, for once they have reached such a stage, there is no need for him to take any further steps. They have become his followers, and they never revolt against his orders, because ignorance goes hand in hand with love of the world. If Eblis should order them to unbelief, they would become unbelievers. In this context, Eblis insinuates himself into them, injecting doubt and temptation concerning that about which God has given indication, entangling them in heresy, and so completes his work.

The Third Manifestation is that in which Eblis appears in the actions of the righteous, where he makes what they do seem beautiful to them, such that they fall prey to self-satisfaction. Now, while he is preparing the way for self-satisfaction to intrude into their souls, so that they become pleased with their actions, Eblis makes them proud about what they believe, so that they reject the advice of any wise person. Once they have arrived at this condition, Eblis tells them, "If others do a hundredth of what you do, they will be saved." As a result, they lessen their efforts and seek after leisure, having an inflated view of themselves and looking down on others. In this state they become ill-natured and suspicious of others, engaging in gossip, so that Eblis is able to convince them to commit any number of sins, one after another, telling them, "Do whatever you want, because God is forgiving and merciful and never punishes anybody," and "God is munificent and is reluctant to punish the elderly," and "It is unthinkable that one who is so munificent would insist on his own rights." Eblis convinces them of this sort of reasoning, so that what they have consecrated to devoutness is replaced by depravity, and affliction is visited upon them.

The Fourth Manifestation concerns intentions and the seeking of superiority in actions. In this manifestation Eblis appears to those who enjoy vision *(shohud)*, in order to pervert their intentions, until their actions, too, are corrupted. While one of them is acting in the way of God, Eblis incites a Satan in his consciousness, telling him, "Improve your actions, for people are watching you, and they might start emulating you!" Now, this occurs when Eblis is unable to influence a person by way of hypocrisy and lust, as was mentioned earlier, saying that "So-and-So is this way and so-and-so is thay way."

If Eblis is unsuccessful in this approach, he approaches the person by way of good intentions, asking him, while he is engaged in a virtuous activity, such as reading the Koran, "Wouldn't it be better if you were to make a pilgrimage to the House of God and read the Koran along the way as much as you can, whereby you would be combining the merit of pilgrimage with that of reading the Koran." He speaks in this way to the person, in order to force him to set forth, and on the way he instills in him such words as "You should be like others; after all, you're on a journey now and a traveller is not required to read the Koran." As a result, the person gives up reading the Koran. Furthermore, because of the inauspiciousness of having done that, he may abandon the very practices which he was required to perform, possibly even give up the pilgrimage altogether. On the other hand, he may simply miss all the requisite rituals of the pilgrimage by spending his time looking for food. Then, very likely, as a result of this, he may develop miserliness, irritability and inertia, and a wealth of other conditions like these. So, one whose actions Eblis is unable to corrupt, is approached through the suggestion of performing better actions, so that he may eventually drop the original activity, and then prove to be unsteady in pursuit of the second, as well.

The Fifth Manifestation is that of knowledge, in which Eblis appears to the wise, causing them to deviate from the way of knowledge. This is the best way of leading them astray.

It is said that Eblis said, "From my point of view it is easier to lead a thousand wise men astray than an illiterate who is strong in his faith, because I remain confounded about what to do about that illiterate of strong faith, whereas, in contrast, misguiding a learned man is easy for me." Thus, Eblis enters and inculcates through the way of knowledge in which the given learned man believes he is right, such that the learned man comes to follow him, and Eblis' position is strengthened. For example, Eblis may tempt one in the area of lust through the way of knowledge, telling the individual, "Marry this woman according to the Jewish rite", although he is a Ḥanafi; or "according to the rite of Abu Ḥanifa, without a sponsor," although the man himself is a Shâfe'i. Then, once the individual has done this and the wife claims the bride-price, wife-support and clothing, Eblis tells him, "Swear to her that you will give her such-and-such in due course and that you will do such-and-such for her, although, of course, you will do nothing of the kind, because it is impermissible for a man to swear to his wife that he will give her satisfaction, even if he swears falsely." Now, if a long time passes, and that woman complains to a judge, Eblis tells him, "Deny that she is your wife, because the contract you made is corrupt from the point of view of your sect and, hence, invalid, so that she is not your wife and, therefore, there is no need to provide wife-support or anything else." As a result, the given learned man swears an oath and proceeds to his own advantage. The variety of these activities is numerous, there being no limit to them, and it is only a very few individuals amongst the outstanding men of the Path who, when exposed to them, manage to keep their souls intact.

The Sixth Manifestation is the one in which Eblis appears to the veracious disciples by perverting their desire for relaxation, leading them into the darkness of animal nature by way of habit and self-indulgence, in order to strip them of their power of aspiration towards seeking, and their intense interest.

When they have lost these, they return to their own selves *(nafs)*, so that Eblis works on them in the same way as he does on others who lack commitment, and there is nothing more threatening to disciples than self-indulgence and yielding to habit.

The Seventh Manifestation is in the course of Divine gnosis, where Eblis appears to the righteous, the friends of God *(auliyâ')* and the gnostics, with the exception of those whom God has protected. Of course, he has no means of approach to God's intimates *(moqarrebân)*. The first way in which Eblis appears to them [the righteous, the *auliyâ'* and the gnostics] is in Reality (*ḥaqiqat*), when he asks them, "Is it not so that God is the Reality of all beings, and that you are a part of beings and therefore God is the Reality of you?" They, in turn, answer, "Yes, it is so." Next, he asks them, "Why do you tire yourselves in doing things which blind followers do?" As a result, they abandon religious actions. Once they have done so, Eblis tells them, "Do what you like, for God is the Reality of you. You are He, and God is above 'why and wherefore' in his actions." Consequently, they indulge in adultery, stealing, drinking, till their deeds lead them to the point where they are utterly stripped of anything of Islam, losing faith and falling into unbelief and heresy.

Some of these come to believe in unification (*etteḥâd*) with God; others actually claim to *be* God. Thereupon, if they are called to account and are summoned to answer for the reprehensible things they have done, Eblis tells them, "Deny all and refuse to submit, because you have done nothing wrong, for what you have done, was done by God. It is simply a matter of what people think you have done, because an oath is sworn according to the intention of someone who has been asked to swear it." As a result, they swear they have done nothing. It may even be the case that Satan communes with them in the guise of God, telling them, "I am God and I have given you permission to perform what is prohibitied; so do as you wish; do such-and-such, however unlawful, and you will have committed no sin."

Of course, none of these things take place, unless Eblis appears to these persons. Otherwise, between God and His devotees there are much more likely to be private communions and mysteries than these sorts of goings on. Moreover, between God and the people of God there are signs which are irrefutable, whereas these signs are unclear to those who are not alert to such, because they are unaware of these principles, otherwise things like these are not hidden from those who possess cognition of the fundamentals. Have you not heard the anecdote about our master, Shaikh 'Abdol'l-Qâder Gilâni, when he was in the desert and was hailed by a voice saying, "O 'Abdo'l-Qâder, I am God and I have made the prohibited things permissible to you; so, do as you wish." He replied, "You are lying! You are Satan!" Later he was asked, "How did you know that that was Satan?" He explained, "God has said, 'God does not command indecency or tell you concerning God such that which you know not.' " (VII:28), so that while that accursed one was telling me to do this, I came to realise that it was Satan, wanting to lead me astray." This is, in fact, the sort of thing that happens to the devotees of God, as to the combatants on the field of Badr[1] and others. This is a condition that I do not deny.

This much suffices to explain the work of Eblis and the variety of his manifestations. If we wish to explain fully and completely the various projections in one of these seven manifestations, we will have to write books and books.

Just as Eblis appears to gnostics at different levels, he may also appear in all these projections to those in the lower levels, but the reverse is not the case. For example, it may be the case for certain gnostics that he appears to them, sometimes in the form of a Divine Name, occasionally in the form of an Attribute, and again, in the form of the Essence, or alternatively, as the Throne, or as the Pedestal, or as the Tablet, or in the form of the Pen, or again *'amâ'*,[2] or as Reality, or as

1. The first battle between the Moslems and their enemies.
2. In Sufi terminology *'ama'* has been defined as: "Inward aspect: 'The dark mist', 'Being', sunk in itself, bare potentiality," and "symbol of the state of Absolute non-manifestation of the Divine Obscurity." See R.A. Nicholson, *Studies in Islamic Mysticism* (Cambridge U. Press., Rp. 1980), p.97, and Burckhardt, *op. cit.* p.59.

a manifestation of the Lofty and an attribute of the Sublime, but only the outstanding friends of God recognise these things for what they are. When such a friend recognises him, that which Eblis wants to use to lead him astray, becomes that which guides him, bringing him closer to the divine presence. Eblis continues doing such things to a friend of God right up to the latter's death, and that friend of God will attain realisation of Divine Truth. Through these things he becomes established in stability (*tamkin*), whereupon the governance of Eblis ceases, and this condition continues till the Day of Judgement. Now the Day of Judgement is none other than the Day of Resurrection and when the gnostic attains the third level of annihilation *(fanâ)*[1] in God, and no trace of him is left, the lesser resurrection occurs to him, the end of which is the Day of Judgement. Now, this is as far as we shall take this explanation, because we cannot disclose the mystery.

Know and be aware that the Satans are the offspring of the accursed Eblis, such that once he has come to dominate the ego of the animal nature, he marries the fire of lusts in the heart to animal habits, from which marriages are born the Satans, just as when sparks fly from the fire or plants spring from the earth. These Satans are the children and followers of Eblis and are present in the form of egoistic thoughts, which lead people astray. It is they who are the "sneaking whisperer" (CXIV:4). It is here that Eblis is a partner with people, such as where God has told Eblis to "be a partner in their property and children." (XVII:62) In certain of the Satans the nature of fire predominates, such that they are linked to the elemental spirits, while for others the vegetable nature comes to dominate, emerging in human form, although they are wholly satanic, as where God has called them the "Satans of man and jinn." (VI:112) Those who appear in human form are Eblis' 'cavalry', being more powerful than Satans, who are limited to spirits; they are the roots of calamity in the world, while the others are the branches thereof, being the infantry of their host, where God has said, "And bring up your horse and foot against

1. Jili defines three levels of annihilation: the first, of self; the second of presence; and the third, of qualities. See Burckhardt, *op. cit.*, p.14.

them." (XVII:64)

Now, know that the most powerful means for Eblis is negligence (*gheflat*), for negligence serves as his sharpest sword. Then there is lust, which, like an arrow, kills by striking the most vulnerable spot. Then there is domination, which is like castles and fortresses, preventing the destruction of Eblis. Further, there is ignorance, which is like a steed, for on it Eblis travels wherever he likes.

EK (J) 39-43

RUMI'S STORY OF MO'AWIYA AND EBLIS

EBLIS' WAKING MO'AWIYA[1] FOR THE MORNING PRAYER

It is recounted that Mo'âwiya was lying asleep in a corner of his palace.

The palace door was bolted from within, for he was tired of people visiting him.

Suddenly a man awoke him; when he opened his eyes the man had disappeared.

He said, "No one was granted entrance to the palace, who could this be who displays such impudence and boldness?"

He started to look around to find a clue of that hidden one.

Behind the door he spied a schemer who was hiding behind a curtain.

"Hey!" he cried, "Who are you? What is your name?" "Simply put," he replied, "my name is Eblis the hardhearted."

He asked, "Why did you take such trouble to waken me? Tell me truly, do not twist your words.

Especially a thief like you, a brigand of the way. Why on earth would you want to be kind to me?"

1. One of the friends of the Prophet who disputed the caliphate with 'Ali.

"The time of prayer is almost up," Eblis said. "You must run quickly to the mosque.

As the Prophet in his wisdom, said, 'Hasten to your devotions before the time has past.' "

"No, no," Mo'âwiya said, "It is not your purpose to guide me to that which is good.

If a thief creeps into my house, and tells me 'I am standing guard',

How can I believe him? What does a thief know of the merit of good works?"

How Eblis Answered Mo'âwiya

"At first I was an angel," said Eblis. "I followed the path of obedience with all my soul.

"I was the intimate of the travellers of the Path, the close companion of the dwellers by the Throne.

Where could the heart's first inclination go? How could the heart's first love depart from the heart?

If, on a journey you see Anatolia or Khotan, how could the love of your own home homeland vacate your heart?

I, too, have been amongst the drunkards of this wine[1]; I have been a lover at His court.

They cut my umbilical in love of Him; they planted love of Him in my soul.

I have seen days of good fortune in my time; I have drunk the water of mercy in springtime.

Was it not His bounteous hand that created me? Was it not He that raised me from nothingness?

Many is the time I have been caressed by Him, and walked in the rose-garden of His contentment.

He would lay the hand of mercy upon my head and let flow from me the fountains of grace.

Who found milk for me in my infancy? Who rocked my cradle? It was He.

What milk did I drink other than His milk?

1. The wine of Divine Unity (*tauḥid*)

What nourished me except His wisdom?

How can the character which entered by way of milk thereafter be separated from one's being?

Though the One whose bounty is like the sea may become wrathful, how could the doors of His bounty ever close?

The substance from which his currency is coined is justice, grace and generosity; wrath is but a powder of alloy on its surface.

Through grace did He make the world; His sun caressed the particles.

If separation is full of His wrath, it's so that union with Him may be appreciated.

Separation rebukes the soul, so that the soul may value the moments of union.

The Prophet declared that God said, 'My aim in creation was beneficence;

I created so that they might benefit from Me, so that they might sample my sweetness.

I did not create to benefit from them, nor to tear clothing from the naked.

In the few days since He drove me from His presence, my eye has remained upon His beauteous face,

How amazing! That such wrath should come from such a face! Everyone is preoccupied with the cause of this.

I do not regard the cause, for that is temporal, and the temporal is caused by the temporal.

I look upon the antecedent grace; whatever is temporal, I tear in two.

I grant that my failure to prostrate was due to envy, but that envy which comes from love, not from denial.

The envy that comes from love arises when another becomes the Beloved's companion.

Jealousy-in-love is the consequence of love, as sure as 'God bless you!' is the consequence of the sneeze.

Since there was only this move on His board, when He said 'Play!', what more could I do?

I played and lost the one game that I had, and threw myself into affliction.

Even in affliction I am savouring his pleasures, I am checkmated by Him! By Him! By Him!

How can anyone break out, O clever one, from this checkmate upon the world's board?

How can a part of the world extricate itself from the whole of the world? Especially when the Unique One makes one's position impossible.

Whoever finds himself in the compass of the world is in the fire; only the creator of the world can liberate him.

Whether in infidelity or faith in Him, you are made by the Lord and belong to Him."

How Mo'âwiya Again Exposes Eblis' Deceit to Him

The Amir said to him, "These things are true, but you are not faultless in all of this.

You have waylaid hundreds of thousands like me, you have tunnelled and entered the treasury.

You are fire and oil; you've no choice but to burn; whose clothes are not torn to shreds by your hand?

Your nature, O fire, is to burn; you can't help it if you set things on fire.

The curse is that He makes you go on burning, and makes you the master of all thieves.

You have talked to God and heard him directly; what am I, O foe, before your deceit?

Your knowledge is like the call of the fowler's whistle; it has the cry of birds, but it is a trap.

It has waylaid hundreds of thousands of birds; the bird is tricked into thinking that a friend has come.

When it hears the sound of the whistle in the air, it comes from the air and is made captive here.

Noah's people lament because of your deceit, their hearts roasted and their breasts torn to shreds

You swept the people of 'Ad[1] away from the world, hurling them into torment and suffering.

From you came the stoning of the people of Lot; because of you they wallowed in the black water.

Through you Nimrod's brain was destroyed, O you who have provoked a myriad of discords!

The intellect of Pharoah, the brilliant philosopher, was confounded by you and deprived of understanding.

Abu Lahab[2] also went bad because of you; the wisest sage turns fool through you.

It is you who, as a lesson, have checkmated a thousand master-players on this chessboard.

With the complicated moves of your queen, you burn our hearts and blacken your own.

You are a sea of trickery, the creatures but drops; you are a very mountain, Solomon is but a particle.

Who escapes your trickery, O adversary? We are drowned in the flood, except those who are protected.[3]

Many an auspicious star has been burnt out by you; many a massed army put to rout by you."

How Eblis Again Replied to Mo'âwiya

Eblis said, "Let me, resolve this problem: I am the touchstone to distinguish counterfeit from true.

God has made me the test of lion and cur; God has made me the test of false coin and true.

When have I tarnished the false coin's face? I am the assayer; I only assess.

For what purpose do I lay out different types of fodder? In order to expose the nature of the beast.

When a wolf gives birth, having mated with a deer, it is uncertain whether its offspring is a deer or a wolf.

1. A tribe mentioned in the Koran who were punished for their transgressions.
2. The first cousin of the Prophet's grandfather, subject of Sura 111, who was the only member of the Prophet's own clan to oppose him.
3. Reference to Koran XI:43.

Drop grass and bones before it, and see which it lunges towards.

If it heads for the bones, it is canine; if it prefers the grass, it is a deer.

From the wrath and mercy of God was born the world of good and evil.

Offer grass or bone; offer food of the soul or food of the ego [*nafs*];

If he is seeking food of the ego, he has no value; if he is seeking food of the spirit, he's a leader.

If he serves the body, he's an ass; if he plunges into the sea of soul, he finds pearls.

Though the inclinations of good and evil are different, they are both involved in the same work.[1]

The Prophets offer devotions, the adversaries offer passions.

How can I turn good to bad? I am not God! I only encourage. I am not their creator.

How can I make fair into foul? I am not the Lord! I am only a mirror for the fair and the foul.

The ugly person, in irritation, smashed his mirror, saying 'This mirror causes a man to look ugly'.

He made me a tattle-tale and a truth-teller, so that I may tell where the fair and the foul are.

I am the witness; jails are not for witnesses; I'm not for prisons, of that God is the witness.

Wherever I see a fruitful sapling, I foster it and nurse it along.

Wherever I see a tree that's stunted and dry, I cut it down, so that the musk is separated from the dung.[2]

The dry tree protests to the gardener, saying, 'Hey, good fellow, why do you cut an innocent down'?

The gardener answers, 'Silence, O ill-favoured one! Is not your dryness sin enough for you?'

The dry tree says, 'I'm straight; I am not crooked; why do you cut the roots of one who is innocent?'

1. Feeding.
2. So that good is separated from bad.

The gardener answers, 'If you had any luck, you'd have been green as well as crooked.

You would have absorbed the water of life; you would have been steeped in it.

Your seed and your root were bad; you were not grafted to sound stock.

If a stunted branch is grafted to a healthy bough, the healthy one will influence its very essence.' "

How Mo'âwiya Berated Eblis

"O brigand," said the Amir, "do not dispute! There's no way you can get to me, don't try.

You're a brigand, and I am a stranger and a merchant; why should I buy the clothes that you bring?

Do not prowl around my goods with bad intentions; you're no customer for anyone's goods.

A brigand is no customer for anyone; if he pretends to be, it's deceit and craft.

What doesn't this envious one have in his pumpkin?[1] O God, deliver us from this enemy's hand!

If he casts one more lot of spells over me, this brigand will steal the shirt off by back!"

How Mo'âwiya Complained about Eblis to God Most High and Appealed for His Help

"O God, this talk of his billows out like smoke; take my hand or my cloak will be all soot!

I cannot match logic in debating Eblis, for he's the seducer of both noble and base.

Adam, who is the manifestation of all the Names,[1] was powerless before the lightning lunge of this cur.

Eblis caused Adam to be flung out of heaven down to the earth; Adam was no more than a fish upon his hook,

1. Head.
2. Reference to Koran II:31.

Crying out, 'We have wronged ourselves'! There is no limit to Eblis' stratagems and guile.

Behind his every statement is mischief; hundreds of thousands of spells are within him.

He strips men of manhood in a moment; he kindles the passions in man and woman.

O Eblis, ruination of people, agitator, why did you wake me? Tell the truth!"

How Eblis Exposed His Deceit Once Again

Eblis said, "No man who thinks ill, will hear the truth despite a hundred signs.

When one who fantasises is presented with reason his fantasies increase.

When one talks to such a person, their words become the very cause of that person's fantasy. The crusader's sword is a tool for a thief.

So the response to him is silence and peace; to talk with an idiot is insanity.

Why do you complain to God of me, O simple one? Complain about the wickedness of your own ignoble ego!

If you eat sweets, you get boils; catch a fever and your health fails.

You curse Eblis, who is innocent; how is it that you don't see that deception is from yourself?

It is not Eblis' fault; it's your own, misguided one, that you are running like a fox for the *donba*[1] of the sheep.

When you see the *donba* in a green meadow, it is a trap. Why do you not realize this?

Your ignorance comes from your craving for the *donba:* it has distanced you from knowledge and blinded both your eye and reason.

Your love of things makes you blind and deafens you; your carnal soul is at fault. Don't pick a fight.

1. Large faty deposits which hang from the hind quarters of a breed of sheep raised in the deserts of the Middle East.

Do not ascribe the guilt to me; do not see things distorted; I have nothing to do with evil, greed or spite.

I did a wrong thing; I still regret it; I wait for my night to turn into day.

Amongst humanity I stand accused; every man and woman lay their sins on me.

The poor old wolf, though hungry, is accused of being well off.

When, because of weakness, he staggers, people say he is dyspeptic from rich food."

How Mo'âwiya Rebutted Eblis with Renewed Insistence

"Only if you speak the truth will you be freed," Mo'âwiya said. "Justice is calling you to truth.

For me to release you, you must tell the truth. Deceit won't settle the dust raised by my scuffling."

"How do you know the difference between truth and falsehood?" asked Eblis, "O you who imagine things and are full of fanciful notions."

Mo'âwiya replied, "The Prophet has provided guidance; he has laid down the touchstone to distinguish the false from the true.

'Falsehood,' he has said, 'is a misgiving in hearts, while truth is a joyous tranquillity.'

The heart finds no peace in lying; water and oil kindle no light.

Truthful talk calms the heart; truths are bait to snare the heart.

If the heart is sickly and unsavoury, it cannot distinguish one taste from another.

Once the heart recuperates from pain and disease, it comes to recognise the taste of falsehood and truth.

When Adam's greed for wheat increased, it plundered his heart of health.

So, he listened to your lying and temptations; he became deceived and drank the poison [of your words].

At that moment he could not tell poison from potion; discrimination flies from one who's drunk with passion.

People are drunk with expectation and desire; they accept your trickery.

Whoever has freed himself from desire, has made his eye familiar with the mystery [of God]."

How Mo'âwiya Brought Eblis to Confess

"So, why did you awaken me? After all you are opposed to awareness, charlatan!

Just like the poppy seed, you make everyone sleep; just like wine, you steal knowledge and reason.

I've pinned you down. Come, tell the truth. I know what is true; play no tricks with me.

I expect from each one the nature and disposition particular to himself.

I do not seek sugar from vinegar, or take a weakling for a soldier.

I do not, like the idolators, look for an idol to be God, or even take it as a sign from God.

I do not seek the smell of musk from dung; I do not look for dry bricks in a river.

From Satan, who is 'other', I do not look for this: That he should waken me for a good cause."

How Eblis Truly Told Mo'âwiya What Was Inside Him

Eblis talked on with deceit and treachery; the Amir heard not, battled on, and held his ground.

Finally, Eblis reluctantly said, "My purpose in waking you was that

You might join the congregation in prayer behind the Prophet of high esteem.

If you had missed the time of prayer, this world would have become dark to you, without illumination.

From disillusionment and pain tears would then have flowed from your eyes, just as water from a water-skin.

Each person takes delight in a particular act of devotion, and cannot bear to miss it, even for a moment.

That disillusionment and pain would have been worth a hundred prayers. What is ritual prayer compared to the feeling of remorse?"

How Eblis Concluded the Confession of His Deceit to Mo'âwiya

Then 'Azâzil said to him, "O Amir, I must confess to you my deceit.

If you had missed your prayers you would have sighed from an aching heart, and cried out, 'Woe!'

That regret, that lamentation and that remorse would have been worth more than two hundred litanies and prayers.

I woke you for fear that such a sigh might burn away the veil.

So that you would not sigh so; so that access to that sigh would be denied.

I am envious; I did this out of envy; I am the enemy; my work is deceit and spite."

Mo'âwiya said, "Now you've told the truth; you're truthful. You are capable of this, it suits you.

You are a spider; you hunt flies; you cur; I am no fly, so don't trouble yourself.

I am a white falcon. It's the King that hunts me; how can a spider weave his web round me?

Go catch flies to your heart's content, invite the flies to have some *dugh.*[1]

And if you offer them honey, that will be lies and *dugh*[2] to boot.

1. A sour drink made from yoghurt.
2. A double play on words; *dugh* rhymes with *dorugh* which means 'lies' and is slang for fraud.

You woke me, but that awakening was really putting me to sleep; you showed me a ship, but in fact it was a maelstrom.

You exhorted me to good, so that you might drive me from a better good."

MM II 2604-793

BIBLIOGRAPHY

Anṣâri, Khwâja 'Abdo'llâh. *Resâl'el jame'-e Khwâja 'Abdo'llâh-e Anṣâri.* Edited by Wahid Dastgerdi. Tehran, 1968.

Arberry, A.J., trans. *The Doctrine of the Sufis.* Partial translation of Kalâbâdhi's *Kitab at-ta'rrof.* Cambridge University Press, 1977.

———. trans. *Muslim Saints and Mystics.* Partial translation of 'Aṭṭâr's *Tadhkerat al-auliyâ'.* London, 1976.

'Aṭṭâr, Farido'd-Din. *Elâhi-nâma.* Edited by Helmut Ritter. Tehran, 1980.

———. *Manteq-o'ṭ-ṭair.* Edited by Seyyed Ṣâdeq Gauharin. Tehran, 1977.

———. *Moṣibat-nâma.* Edited by Nurâni Weṣal. Tehran, 1977.

———. *Tadhkerat al-auliyâ'.* Edited by Moḥammad Este'lâmi. Tehran, 1975.

Bokhârâ'i, 'Abdo'llâh Mostamli. *Sharḥ-e ta'arrof.* Edited by Aḥmad 'Ali Rajâ'i. Tehran, 1970.

Ebn 'Arabi, Moḥyiyo'd-Din. *Sharḥ-e kalemât-e ṣufiya az Moḥyiyo'd- Din ebn 'Arabi.* Edited by Maḥmud Maḥmudo'l-Ghorâb. Damascus, 1981.

———. *The Tarjumân al-Ashwaq:* A Collection of Mystical Odes by Muhyi'ddin ibn al-'Arabi. Edited and trans. by R.A. Nicholson. Reprint: 1911; London, 1978.

'Erâqi, Fakhro'd-Din Ebrâhim. *Kolliyât-e 'Erâqi.* Edited by Sa'id Nafisi. Tehran, 1959.

Ghazâli, Aḥmad. *Majmu'a-ye âthâr-e fârsi-ye Aḥmad-e Ghazâli.* Edited by Aḥmad Mojâhed. Tehran, 1979.

———. *Resâla-ye sawâneh wa resâla'i dar mau'eẓa.* Edited by Dr. Javad Nurbakhsh. Tehran, 1973.

Ḥallâj, Ḥosain ebn Manṣur. *Kitab al-Ṭawasin.* Edited with

notes, commentary and indexes by Louis Massignon. Paris, 1913.

———. *The Ṭawasin of Manṣur al-Ḥallaj.* Trans. Aisha Abd ar- Rahman at-Tarjumana. Berkeley and London, 1974.

Hamadâni, ‘Aino’l-Qoḍhât. *Nâmahâ-ye ‘Aino’l-Qoḍhât-e Hamadâni.* Edited by ‘Ali-Naqi Manzawi and ‘Afif ‘Osairân. Tehran, 1969.

———. *Tamhidât.* Edited by ‘Afif ‘Osairân, Tehran, 1962.

Hojwiri, ‘Ali ebn ‘Othmân. *Kashf al-maḥjub.* Edited by V.A. Zhukovsky. Leningrad, 1926.

———. *Kashf al-Maḥjub of Al Hujwiri: The Oldest Persian Treatise on Sufism.* Trans. R.A. Nicholson, E.J.W. Gibb Memorial Series Vol. 17. Reprint: 1911, London 1976.

Jâmi, ‘Abdo’r-Raḥmân. *Haft aurang.* Edited by Morteḍhâ Gilâni. Tehran, 1978.

Jili, ‘Abdo’l-Karim al-. *Al-ensân al-kâmel.* Cairo, 1886.

———. *Universal Man.* Extracts from *Al-ensân al-kâmel.* English trans. by Angela Culme-Seymour from the French trans. of the Arabic by Titus Burckhardt. UK: Beshara Publications, 1983.

Kolaini, Moḥammad ebn Ya‘qub. *Osul-e kâfi.* Edited and trans. by Jawâd Moṣṭafawi. Shiraz, 1980.

Maibodi, Abo’l-Faḍhl Rashido’d-Din. *Kashf al-asrâr wa ‘oddat al- abrâr ma‘ruf ba tafsir-e Khwâja ‘Abdo’llâh ‘Anṣâri.* 10 Vols. Edited by ‘Ali Asghar Ḥekmat. Tehran 1978.

Massignon, Louis, *Moṣâ’-eb-e Ḥallâj.* Trans. from French into Persian by Dr Seyyed Dhiya’od-Din Dehshiri. Tehran, n.d.

———. *The Passion of Ḥallaj: Mystic of Islam.* Trans. by Herbert Mason. 4. Vols. Princetown, U.S.A., 1982.

Nasafi, ‘Azizo’d-Din, *Ketâb-e ensân-e kâmel.* Edited by Marijan Molé. Tehran and Paris, 1962.

Nâṣer Khosrau. *Diwân-e Nâṣer Khosrau wa roshanâ’i nama wa sa‘âdat-nâma-e.* Edited by Mojtabâ Minowi. Tehran, 1928.

Ne‘mato’llâh Wali, Shâh. *Rasâlahâ-ye Shah Ne‘mato’llâh-e Wali.* Edited by Dr. Javad Nurbakhsh. Tehran, 1978.

Nicholson, R.A. *Studies in Islamic Mysticism.* Reprint: 1921, Cambridge U. Press, 1980.

Qoshairi, Abo’l-Qâsem. *Tarjoma-ye resâla-ye Qoshairiya.* Edited and trans. by Badi‘oz-Zamân Foruzanfâr. Tehran, 1982.

Rumi, Jalâlo'd-Din. *Mathnawi-ye ma'nawi*. Edited by R. A. Nicholson. Tehran 1977.

____. *The Mathnawi of Jalâlu'ddin Rumi*. Edited and translated by R.A. Nicholson. 3 Vols. 4th edition. London, 1977.

Ruzbehân Baqli Shirâzi. *Mashrab al-arwâḥ*. Turkey, n.d.

____. *Sharḥ-e shaṭḥiyât*. Edited, notes, introduction and indexes by Henry Corbin. Tehran, 1981.

Sabzawâri, Hâjj Mollâ Hâdi, *Diwân-e Asrâr*. Edited by Seyyed Moḥammad Reḍha Dâ'i-Jawâd. Eṣfahân, n.d.

Sa'di, Maṣlaḥo'd-Din. *Bustân*. Edited by Moḥammad-'Ali Forugh. Tehran, 1978.

Sanâ'i, Abo-'l-Majd Majdud. *Diwân*. Edited by Modarres Raḍhawi. Tehran, 1975.

INDEX OF KORANIC QUOTATIONS

GENERAL INDEX